POETRY MATTERS

Edited by Mark Richardson

Poems From The South

First published in Great Britain in 2011 by:

 Young**Writers**

Young Writers
Remus House
Coltsfoot Drive
Peterborough
PE2 9BF
Telephone: 01733 890066
Website: www.youngwriters.co.uk

Foreword

Since our inception in 1991, Young Writers has endeavoured
to promote poetry and creative writing within schools by
running annual nationwide competitions. These competitions
are designed to develop and nurture the burgeoning creativity
of the next generation, and give them valuable confidence in
their own abilities.

This regional anthology is one of the series produced by our
latest secondary school competition, *Poetry Matters*.
Using poetry as their tool, the young writers were given the
opportunity to tell the world what matters to them. The authors
of our favourite three poems were also given the chance to
appear on the front cover of their region's collection.

Whilst skilfully conveying their opinions through poetry, the
writers showcased in this collection have simultaneously
managed to give poetry a breath of fresh air, brought it to life
and made it relevant to them. Using a variety of themes and
styles, our featured poets leave a lasting impression of their
inner thoughts and feelings, making this anthology a rare
insight into the next generation.

Contents

Bloxham School. Banbury

Oliver Pelendrides [16] 1
George Baker [14] 1
Harry Coward [14]..2
George Herbert [14] 2
Oliver Johnson [14] 3

Broadwater School, Godalming

Chanice Edwards [12] 3
Kathryn Redrup [13] 4
Kyarah Helen Betker [13] 5
Carmen Fitzmaurice [15]...6
Angus Fitzsimmons [11] 6
Raven Habgood Brown [11] 7
Aaron Burt [11]...7
Jade Ford [12] 8
Oliver Dunn [11] 8
Jevon Napper [11] 9
Kaloyan Batalov [12] 10
Anna Bradshaw [11] 10
Simon Clark [12]...11
Simona Stefanova [11] 11
George Hale [12]...12
Aaron Storey [12] 12
Jennifer Squire [12] 13
Danielle Fulker [11] 13
Nathan Morris [11] 14
Cameron Thomson [11] 14

Carterton Community College, Carterton

Chloe Moscrop [11] 14
Megan Cole [12]...15
Megan Rockett [13]...16
Bethany Mathias [12] 17
Phoebe Croxford [11] 18
Rachael Tozer [13] 19

Logan Prové [11] 20
Zoe Haydon [11]...21
Libby Exley [11] 22
Natasha Rudge [12]..22
Henry Stephens [11] 23
Thomas Dickinson [14] 23
Rebecca Sanderson [12] 24
Dylan Moyce [12] 25
Chloe King [12]...26
Megan Pearson [13] 26
Aimee Felstead [13] 27
Chloe Wingrove [13]..27
Alysia Anderton [11] 28
Sophie Brain [13]..28
Ellen Moore [14] 29
Bethan Milner [12] 29
Chloe Wiblin [13] 30
Amber Exley [13] 30
Tierney Kelman [11] 31
Vicky Bakula [12] 31
Lucy Grisman & Lois Smith 32
Tom Hurren [13] 32
Liam Morris [13]..33
Torin Harley [13]..33

Etonbury Middle School, Arlesey

Charmaine Smethurst [10] 34
Talena Day [12] 35
Ella Burns [11] 36
Kayleigh Little [10]..36
Dylan Joseph [13] 37
Alice Page [12] 37
Emma Boughton [11] 38
Rhiannon Mackie [12]..39
Niamh Coughlan [11] 39
Maya Dhaliwal [11] 40

Farnham Heath End School, Farnham
James Anthony Traylen [14] 41

Fitzwaryn School, Wantage
William Moffett [14] 41
Chantell Moffatt [15] 42
Brett Hemingway [15] 42

Gosden House School, Guildford
Lorna Freestone [13] 43
Jessica Short [13] 43
Hannah Kemp [13] 44
Katarina Feroce [13] 44
Yeukai Kamoto [13] 45
Courtney Chedd [13] 45
Rachel Livingstone [13] 46

Havant College, Havant
Joe McQuilken [16] 46
Tom Pickard [16] 47
Nadia Evering [17] 48
Maza Kebede [16] 49
Bella Sanderson [17] 50
Kaubo Axell Muyembe [17] 51
Emma Durham [17] 52
Tom Crease [17] 52

Hemdean House School, Reading
Lauryn Jackman [11] 53
Monique Skeete [13] 54
Poppy Moroney [14] 54
Ellie Chapman [13] 55
Charlie Pembroke [11] 55
Phoebe Powell [13] 56
Corrie Knowles [13] 56
Stephanie Robinson [12] 57
Georgia Doran [13] 57
Tilly Wallace [11] 58
Lucy Harris [13] 58
Safiya Hussain [12] 59
Sophie Harris [13] 59

Leighton Park School, Reading
Eve Pearson [13] 60
Greta Kitch [11] 60
Max Jennings [12] 61
Mahlah Catline [11] 61
Finbar Aherne [12] 62
Gilly Hines [11] 62
Aimee Fullbrook [14] 63
Scott Morgan 63
Emilia Dixon [11] 64
Victoria Roberts [13] 64
Will Likely [12] 65
Ben Pearson [11] 65
Joe Hadman [11] 65
Charlie Hopkinson [13] 66
Rawdie Marks [11] 66
Will Lewis [13] 66
Max Parfitt [12] 67

Luckley Oakfield School, Wokingham
Jessica Vevers [12] 67
Jessica Arnold 68
Brittany Meakin [12] 69
Lottiey Boyd 70
Ellie Angus [12] 71
Amy Martin [12] 72
Milly Golightly [12] 73
Sophie Bryson [12] 74
Minami Ishii 75
Catherine Tren [12] 76
Aleanor Bakes [12] 77
Claudia Hughes [13] 78
Gaia Webb [12] 78
Lily Andrews [12] 79
Safiah Fraser [12] 79
Emily Clayton 80
Sofia Burchell [12] 80
Lucie Smith [12] 81
Scarlett Markham [12] 82
May Sako [13] 83

Luton Sixth Form College, Luton

Asha Khatun [16] 84
Arooj Javaid Khan Lodhi [16] 85

Mayfield Secondary School, Portsmouth

Katie Downer [14] 86
Jessica Lyn Bonsall [14] 87
Lenny Whelan [11] 88
Rosie Lunn [13] 89
Lauren Sharpe [12] 90
Oliver Hurst [15] 91
Brooke Critchett [11] 91
Shawnie Guy [13] 92

Mount Grace School, Potters Bar

Rachel Dixon [13] 92
Trey Thomas [13] 93
Sarah Evans [13] 94
Katie Scales [13] 95
Sammi Patterson [13] 96
Macey Reynolds [14] 97
Emily Toye [13] 98
Hadley Caswell [13] 99
Nicholas Stringer [13] 99
Maria Harris [13] 100
Emily Allen [13] 100
Maisie Clancy [13] 101
Amy Lawrence [13] 101
Amber Laing [13] 102
Chiara Merlo [13] 103
Emily Pack [13] 104
Hannah Crick [13] 104

Oxford High School, Oxford

Tamara Stojanovic [16] 105
Laura Rosenheim [12] 106
Poppy Simmonds [17] 107

Peter Symonds College, Winchester

Abigail Gibbs [17] 108

Prior's Field School, Godalming

Julia Parison [14] 109
Caitlin McConnell [16] 110
Genevieve Lebus [12] 111
Emily Milton [14] 112
Elena Georgiakakis [12] 113
Jasmine Smith [14] 114
Rebeccah Webber [14] 125
Holly James [13] 126
Kate Alexander [14] 127
Chesca Loggia [13] 127
Lucy Edwards [12] 128
Kimi Worsdell [14] 129
Rebecca Gwyther [13] 129
Alicia Newland [12] 130
Emma Louise Pudge [14] 130
Poppy McGrath [14] 131
Lucy Collecott [12] 132
Sophie Rafter [13] 133
Melissa Price [14] 134
Mariam Hussein [14] 134
Yolanda Foo [13] 135
Maddy Simmonds [12] 135
Elektra Georgiakakis [14] 136
Ashley Davies [12] 137
Georgina Cave [13] 138
Anna Blades [13] 138
Molly D'Angelo [14] 139
Sophie Roberts [12] 139
Charlie Sullivan [15] 140
Hannah Walker [12] 140

Rye St Antony School, Oxford

Katie Abson [11] 141
Minnie Anderson [11] 142
Tilly O'Shea [11] 143
Olivia Purvis [11] 144
Catherine Dorrian & Alice Mitchell [11] 144
Iman Abdel-Haq [11] 145

Lucy Ramsden [11] 145
Sarah Horsfall [12] 146

St Bernadette's Catholic Secondary School, Bristol

Vienna Sheridan [11] 146
Taylor Channing [12] 147
Monica Elsworth [12] 148
Georgia Ponting [13] 149
Paige Coxon [121] 149
Frances Bridgman [11] 150
Sean Noonan [12] 150
Alice O'Farrell [12] 151
Calum Rogers [12] 151
Amelia Bettesworth [11] 152
Alexandra Joan Connell [12] 152
Kira Thomas [11]..................................153
Jerlen Pangilinan [13] 153
Frederick Pearce [12] 154
Josh McQuaid [11] 154
Lewis Rogers [11] 155
Neve McDonnell [11] 155
Ellie Daly [13] 156
Lauryn Duffy [11].................................156
Safiyyah Abdul-Karim [12] 157
Millie Meacham [11] 157
Storm Hanks [13]..................................158
Saul Pitter [12] 158
Shani Avery [12] 159
Michael Morgan [11] 159
Jeffrey Grimes [11]...............................160
Ellie Marie Hodges [12] 160
Anna Korba [13]...................................160
Isaac Parker [12] 161
Regan Sollars [12] 161

St Paul's Catholic College, Sunbury on Thames

Rebecca Coolahan [12].............................161
Ryan Harris Conyard [11] 162
William Souza [11]................................162

Alexandra Wilson [11] 163
Rebecca McGovern [12] 163

The Gregg School, Southampton

Joshua Arnell [13] 163
Felicity Heath [11] 164
Victoria Regan [13] 165
Ross Castle [14] 166
Rebecca Fogden [11]...............................167
Tabitha Hunt [13] 168
Olivia Douglas [13]...............................169
Arman Shabgard [12] 170
Jennifer Burnage [14].............................171
Euan Anderson [15] 172
Jamie Bushnell [14] 173
Charlotte Millman [12] 174
Thomas Captain [11] 175
George Bareham [11] 175
Andrew Heath [13].................................176
Tara Norris [13] 176
Claire Humby [13] 177
William Gray [12] 177
Amber Holland [12] 178
Alexander Chessell [12] 178
Charlotte Bull [14] 179
Greg Anderson [13] 179
Sophie Barnard [11] 180
Dominick Levoi [14] 180
Addison Vincent [12] 181
Joe D'Souza [14] 181
Emma Birch [13] 182
James Atkinson [11] 182
Lauren Scappaticci [11]...........................183
Nathan Thomas [13] 183
Holly Mumford [12] 184
Andrew Pimm [11]..................................184
Ben Woodley [12] 185
Wyatt Brennan [11] 185

The Matthew Arnold School, Staines

Roman Malin [13]....................................186
Jay Simpson [14]....................................186
Mona Gholami [13] 187
Debbie Hawthorn [11] 187
Anesha Tarapdar 188
Lauren Clarey [11] 188
Josie Evans [12] 189
Lauren Farrell [11] & Charlotte Evans.......189
Tom Brock...190
Maisie Marshall [12]..............................190
Jemma Dique [11] 191
Lewis Demmon [12]................................191
Alex Hanson [12] 191
Zeyn Sadiq [11] 192
Phoebe Saville [11].................................192
Rebecca Aldred [13] 193
Katie Clarke [12] 193
Ben Castleman [12].................................194
Rosie Saunders [12] 194
Jessica Ketchen.....................................194

The Tiffin Girls' School, Kingston-upon-Thames

Rachel Tookey [17] 195

Thornden School, Eastleigh

Rosie Upton [13] 196
Adam Rogers [12] 197
Lauren Baverstock [14]...........................198
Alexandra Hopwood [13] 199
Katy Rowledge [12] 200
Lisa Wright [13]....................................200
Amy Crockford [13] 201
Bryony Peters [12] 201
Finlay Naylor [11] 202
James Elliott [12]..................................202
Kirsty McCulloch [12] 203
Lydia Pallot [12]....................................203

Wilson's School, Wallington

Darren Mindham [16]..............................204

Woodland Middle School, Bedford

Martin Lindill [12]................................205
Thomas Herbert [12]..............................206
Kerry Meredith [12]...............................210
Alex Sanderson [12] 212
Charlie Hughes [11]...............................213
Kerry Meredith [12]...............................214
Alex Evans [12] 216
Louis Brown [12] 217
Lucy Pedder [12]....................................218
Thomas Woodcraft [12]...........................219
Michael Frost [11] 220
Jessica Hutchinson [12]..........................221
Millie De Kauwe [12] 222
Lauren Ash [12] 223
Hannah Tyler [12] 224
Jodie Darvall [11]...................................224
Jake Shawe [12] 225
Trudie Reardon [13]................................225
Sasha Ralević [12] 226
George Roberts [12] 226
Regan Ovendale [12] 227
Gemma Scott [11] 227
Rebecca Mair [11] 228
Jack James [11] 228
Thomas Lark [12] 229
Katie Manners [12] 229
Hannah Burdett [12]...............................230
Dom Maelzer [11] 230
Oliver Barker [11] 231
James Tobin [11] 231
Vicky Haimes [12] 232
Jade Burles [12].....................................232
Lucy Guerrero [11] 233
Lois Johnson [12] 233
Mei-Ann Bartram [11].............................234

Emily Potts [11] 234

Ross Knight [13] 235

Elliott Griffett [12] 235

Drew Gillespie [12] 235

Jack Sharp [12] 236

Rhianne Jones [12] 236

Georgia Fleet-Chapman [12] 237

Ben Short [12] 237

Karly Billimore [11] 237

The Poems

The Pity Of Home

She sails in, borne on infinite black,
She turns her sweet face towards Earth,
Her face, so happy and yet not home,
Amongst the planets,
She has turned here millennia,
Yet she feels more akin to the sun,
The stars,
The planets,
She will not burn out, she will not fade,
She pities home, it will go, unlike her,
Her coldness shall be as warmth to her heart when all are gone,
She will observe forever,
She will remember how, once, it was perfect,
She is cold and dark, devoid of life,
She'll be grateful for her coldness, she won't burn up,
Yet she knows home has gone
And she can never return
Home.

Oliver Pelendrides (16)
Bloxham School. Banbury

Leaving Home

We drive away,
The beautiful building, my only home till now,
I look back one last time,
It disappears through the gushing trees,
I look back once more.

I sob on the way,
Thinking only about the home which has made my life,
I think of my adventures I had there,
I will remember everything about there,
The wind blows, I look back along the dusty trail.

George Baker (14)
Bloxham School. Banbury

Building A Home

Open out the door with music
Fastens up the sides of bacon
Polish the windows with the shine of water
Stick on the roof with stone from the country
Arrange the furniture with light from the fire
Squeeze the paint with the energy of a child
Stick on the doorbell, like you made a sandwich
Fill with the smell of Christmas pudding
Put your dog onto the green grass
Carry yourself in with a well deserved cuppa.

Harry Coward [14]
Bloxham School. Banbury

Building A Home

I saw up the brown bark oak from the Amazon
I arrange the blood-red bricks
I line up the lemon yellow diggers
I polish the new, cream marble floor
I squeeze in the dark, black, dirty, bold dishwasher
I colour the walls snow white
I carry in a wintry whisper from outside
I fill my time by sitting in my old, orange, rusty van,
drinking pale, horrible tea.

George Herbert [14]
Bloxham School. Banbury

New Homes

As they stick on the bricks
Polish the wood
Paint the walls
Fill the pool
Screw together the floorboards
Lay down the carpet
I am coming
To see my new house.

Oliver Johnson [14]
Bloxham School. Banbury

Fantastic Fireworks

I stood there in the crowd, thinking
It's cold!
Then a gush of warmth took over.
The gorgeous fireworks made me smile
As if they were made for me.
The bonfire was enormous,
Like an elephant,
The fire made me want to put marshmallows on a stick
And eat them.
I smelt the hotdogs,
So I went and brought one and poured ketchup
All over it.
The fireworks were all different colours
Like . . .
Red - blue - purple
Green - orange - pink
Silver -
They were lovely colours.

Chanice Edwards [12]
Broadwater School, Godalming

Friendship Fading

The honesty we shared
The fun we had
Your were kind, loyal
The best
You supported me
Through thick and thin
But where did it all go?

I felt I was losing grip
Reading a closed book
The fun fading
The emptiness
The trust was gone
I was dying inside
Why couldn't you see?

Now you're gone
The sadness fills me
It was a stabbing pain
I'm lonely
I can't believe this happened
To you, to me, to us
Why did this happen?

As time goes by
You slowly come back
But I've moved on
I'm sorry
You hurt me once
I'm not going to risk it.

I think this is goodbye.

Kathryn Redrup [13]
Broadwater School, Godalming

The Journey

(My granny fought in her own gigantic war and she won in her own way. So here is a poem dedicated to her. I hope you agree that she was a fantastic, wonderful and much admired lady.)

A light shone brightly, from way, way above
And all that was given was pure, powerful love.

Then all of the darkness faded and the room disappeared,
My granny's body was released, away from the pain that she feared.

She was free once again and she could do as she wished
And as no one was watching she blew a goodbye kiss.

Then suddenly, from out of the blue, a carriage arrived,
Which contained a splendid surprise.

As it came to a halt, our grandfather came out,
She was so delighted she gave a big shout.

So off they went, hand in hand,
Into a place where they now proudly stand.

Once they were there a celebration started
And my granny soon felt very light-hearted.

That celebration was out of sadness,
It was a celebration of life and happiness.

My granny shone brighter than the sun or the moon,
She was an angel in Heaven and lit up the room.

That day a journey had begun,
A journey of new life and journey full of fun.

Kyarah Helen Betker [13]
Broadwater School, Godalming

Someone Special

There is something that I have to share
A feeling inside that I can no longer bear
I have to tell of this sensational love
Expressed from a distance above
A love that stirs with laughter, with cry
It's a feeling that cannot be a lie
This joyful expression, so hard to explain
So unusual, it has to be exclaimed
My heart aches for this tender love
That is shown from above
This is not just an ordinary feeling
It's like a strong rush of healing
It's like and electrical impulse sent through my veins
That takes control and releases all my pain
A warmth and comforting presence
Wrapping me with endless guidance
So wonderful that it lifts me up
Above the clouds and the world's dust
High enough, as if I'm flying
So wonderful that I'm crying
This feeling bubbles out of me
It's uncontrollable, I feel like I'm free
Nothing can stop me from feeling this touch
It's never enough, you can never get too much.

Carmen Fitzmaurice (15)
Broadwater School, Godalming

The Car

The car tyres crunched on the gravel,
The car went beep in traffic
The car engines roared
The car brakes squealed in the rain.

Angus Fitzsimmons (11)
Broadwater School, Godalming

The Hit Of Love

Have you ever
Felt love
Maybe from Heaven
Or up above

Love is something
You feel inside
Like a stomach ache
Or butterflies

Your heart feels like
It's gonna pop
Will the feeling
Ever stop?

It is like floating
On a cloud of hope
Sometimes you just
Cannot cope

As I come to the end
Of my rhyme
I hope you will find
True love sometime.

Raven Habgood Brown (11)
Broadwater School, Godalming

The Sailing Boat

The sea swished
As the boat sailed
Across the drumming waves.

The boat's whistle
Echoed through
The crunching tide.

Aaron Burt (11)
Broadwater School, Godalming

The Storm

Walking home one night
Walking with the stormy kite
The rain was pouring down
As the clouds went round and round

As the daylight came
The storm was still the same
On my way to school
It was very cool

As the thunder cracked
You could see the bats
The weather wept
My shoes squeaked as I stepped

As the lightning sparked
It was like we were on Noah's Ark
The night came again
The storm was still the same

The lightning flashed
As the rain splashed
I know there's hope the storm will pass
If it will stay, should I ask?

Jade Ford (12)
Broadwater School, Godalming

Deadbeat

Crash! The floor smashed
The wood exploded under my feet
Snap! Went my legs
Pop! My eye shot out
Thud! It hit the wall
Boom! I'm dead!

Oliver Dunn (11)
Broadwater School, Godalming

The Creepy Crawly Clonk

The creepy crawly clonk
Made the aliens' guns go zonk
And it made their ship go jonk
So the traffic all went honk.

The clonk jumped for joy
But the troublesome traffic went oi!
Then came out a boy
And beat him with a terrible toy.

The clonk fell to the ground
And thought he was in Heaven because of the sound
But it was just a siren wailing
And the clonk thought he was in sunny Spain sailing.

The clonk woke up in his bed
And the doctor said he'd hit his head
And the next thing he said
Was he wanted a bright, shiny shed.

So finally the clonk had his drop in
Fell into his own coffin
Looked up and thought he saw a boffin
But it was a puffin eating a muffin.

Jevon Napper [11]
Broadwater School, Godalming

Pirate Poem

Former pirate, Robert Tough,
One day thought *I've had enough of being tough!*
I would rather like to be
Someone nice, like honeybee.
No more rum and fat cigars
No more skulls and bones and scars
No more wooden legs and hooks
Leave all this in dusty books.

Former pirate, Robert Tough
Threw away his scary stuff
Shaved his beard, sold his parrot
Left his treasure chest to rot
Even learned to smile a lot
And without a second thought
Changed his name to . . . Robert Soft.

Kaloyan Batalov (12)
Broadwater School, Godalming

Dinosaur Poem

In the time before man
Dinos swam, flew and ran
We fought and raced and raced and fought
It would last forever, or so we thought

But then the meteor came
It ended our time with fiery rain
Only rodents in caves survived
All us brilliant dinosaurs died

Think of all a dino's seen
Now there are flats where caves have been
When the wheel had just been found
We were lying in the ground.

Anna Bradshaw (11)
Broadwater School, Godalming

Love

If I have learnt one thing this year
It's that I love you and want you near.
I think of you so very much,
I think of your kisses and your touch.
I think of life, how it would be,
If for some reason you weren't with me.

I know I would surely die,
The very thought makes me cry.
How much I love you I hope you know,
As I try my best to let it show.
Even if we were apart,
Always know you're in my heart.

Simon Clark [12]
Broadwater School, Godalming

The Dark World

Lost, alone, trying to get me way out of this world,
There are dark clouds all around,
No light, just darkness.
The hills aren't bright, they are dark and cold,
No animal lives on them, nothing.
A dark flower makes a little girl have a cold heart.
Nothing, nothing can be seen.
Just a little tear from the little girl's eye.
The cold piano goes silent
And everything
Stops.

Simona Stefanova [11]
Broadwater School, Godalming

The Winter Night

Falling snow from the sky
As the moon was shining
Ice sticks shaped as eyes
As the moon was shining
A little snow gift, just for me
As the moon was shining
A cold place with no glee
As the moon was shining

Old memories, filled with sadness
As the world came down.

George Hale (12)
Broadwater School, Godalming

My Little Brother

My little brother's eyes
Are like the shimmery Northern Lights
His face is like
A newborn kitten
His hair is as blond
As a lion's mane
His personality
Is like a chirpy cub
His skin is
As smooth as a leather sofa.

Aaron Storey (12)
Broadwater School, Godalming

Swimming

Swimming is fun
Even though you can't eat buns!
The water is sometimes hot
The coach has lost the plot!
The water is sometimes cold
But there is always something to hold
I love to swim
But I also like to win!
I can dive really well
And I want to have a bell.

Jennifer Squire [12]
Broadwater School, Godalming

Nonsense

The wind whispered in my ear,
Whilst the bangs sang.
Then a harvest mouse went scampering by
With a crafty claw and a brown eye.

The world around me started to move
And all the frogs squeaked.
The trees sang in tune
To the birds
And the grass crunched underneath my feet.

Danielle Fulker [11]
Broadwater School, Godalming

Animal Antics

Funky Monkey swings in the tree
Until he fell and hurt his knee,
We rushed him off to hospital
Where they quickly sent him to A & E.

Slimy Snake baked a cake
And burnt his skin on a tin,
He put his tail in and pail and drenched it in the water
But instead his skin shed
And with no clothes on he went to bed.

Nathan Morris (11)
Broadwater School, Godalming

Splodge

His hop reminds me of a spring day.
His fur is like a layer of pure, white snow.
His black spots trickle down his sides.
The black line down his back is like the Earth's equator.
When stretched out, he is as long as a doorway.
When alerted by something,
His ears pop up as quick as lightning.

He is my . . . rabbit!

Cameron Thomson (11)
Broadwater School, Godalming

Baby

B arely breathing
A dorable in her sleep
B awling at night and
Y awning in the morning.

Chloe Moscrop (11)
Carterton Community College, Carterton

14

Dance Contest

Hair tied up in a tight bun,
Make-up and glitter all over the place.
Sparkly dresses like mini-skirts,
Looking forward to the day ahead.

Sitting in the car for a long one-hour journey,
Flo Rida's tunes blasting through my ears.
Practising routines in my head,
Getting slightly nervous now.

As the hall comes into sight,
The butterflies wake up in my stomach.
Hundreds of cars here and there,
Parents and children lined up to get in.
As I come up to the door,
I don't want to enter.

Inside the hall, preparing for the performance,
Warming up and stretching with my friends,
Talking about how nervous we are.
I get my number pinned onto my dress
All lines and ready to go,
And then . . .
They call my name,
Here I go, this is it,
Step into the spotlight.
Heart pounding faster than a cheetah's run,
Panicking that I'll mess up.
Music starts . . . and I'm off.

After two minutes the routine's over . . .
Hoping to get a good grade,
As I get presented my trophy
A rush of achievement floods through my veins,
All the butterflies fly away.

Megan Cole (12)
Carterton Community College, Carterton

Friendship

Friendship - what does it mean to me?
What do you tell them? What you've heard, what you've seen?
Well. I'll tell you what I think, but don't act so keen,
I'm only telling you what friendship can mean.

Friendship can be trust,
Telling somebody something that no one else can know,
Not spreading rubbish around, back and forth, to and fro,
But saying, 'Hey, no prob! I'm only going to tell my fluffy, little pillow'
Yeah, that friendship is a must.

Friendship is like a song,
It has high notes and low notes,
It can be very loud or so quiet that it floats,
Or it can be so good that there's always someone who gloats
And if you think that's sill, I strongly believe you're wrong.

Friendship is like a blade of grass,
Has some close friends and ones that live further away
And you're so close to some every second of every day.
So get to know people more, don't be keeping them at bay,
Because that precious moment that you may have,
Very soon may pass.
Whoosh!

Right, I think you know what friendship means to me,
But don't even say things like 'Go on, take a bow!'
Because it just came to me and I don't know how.
But I'm glad I got the chance to tell somebody about friendship,
Properly, finally.

Megan Rockett (13)
Carterton Community College, Carterton

7KD Sends A Postcard Home

(Inspired by 'A Martian Sends A Postcard Home' by Craig Raine)

Playful yes, but many get told not to,
Comfy and soft, cuddly when dark,
Pushed up against the wall,
Need to make it every day.

Black and stiff, cold and solid,
Different shapes and sizes,
The back looks weird in a way,
Picture after picture.

Petite and soft, mild and cosy,
Tucked up really neatly,
Some have several layers,
Females love them.

Humans are obsessed with this greasy stuff,
We see them non-stop eating,
On this planet some die because of it,
Hot or cold, yucky or nice, it may run away.

Pressed on things humans wear,
Hot air and steam appear from it,
Prevents creases,
Then put away in a cupboard to air out.

Warm and white,
Would sometimes char if you touch it,
May sometimes be cool if not turned on,
If you're cold it can help.

Bethany Mathias (12)
Carterton Community College, Carterton

7KD Sends A Postcard Home

(Inspired by 'A Martian Sends A Postcard Home' by Craig Raine)

A minute box with an unlimited memory,
Each one has a different code
Which has to be shared to use it,
Each one has a different melody,
Every day a different face.

Humans are obsessed with this greasy stuff,
We see them non-stop eating,
On this planet,
We see some die because of it,
Hot or cold, yucky or nice,
It might even run away.

Humans scream when they're on this,
There's a thrill round every corner on this planet,
We some cry on it
Because of its up and downs,
Left and right, round and splash,
They might even go again.

People walk there, loud and proud,
With their shirts tucked in and they're all neat.
A bell goes every period,
'Don't be late,' they shout
Or a punishment will be handed out.

Phoebe Croxford (11)
Carterton Community College, Carterton

My Little Box Of Treasures

My little box of treasures
Is filled with things galore

Emotions, memories, favourite things
Friends and family and more

A golden silhouette is shining
Courageous and standing proud

The horse of my dreams approaches me
His whinnies and neighs echo loud

Inside are laughs of comforting joy
And puddles of poignant tears

These which have been gathered
Throughout my previous thirteen years

My box is plated with the finest gold
With millions of diamonds engraved

Shimmering in the sunlight
For many it's certain to be craved

My little box of treasures
Is locked with a sacred key

Emotions, memories, favourite things
Are all that matter to me!

Rachael Tozer [13]
Carterton Community College, Carterton

7KD Sends A Postcard Home

(Inspired by 'A Martian Sends A Postcard Home' by Craig Raine)

On this planet
They have these minute boxes with unlimited memory
Each one has a unique code, which must be shared to use
They each have a different melody
Every day a new voice

On this planet
They have these white porcelain 'bowls'
Which relieve you of your discomfort
Down the water slide it goes
Never to be seen again

On this planet
They have these small, silver boxes
Which attach to plastic balls
Connected by thin cables
They bring music for the humans' delight

On this planet,
They have these wooden sticks
With metallic strings
And each sings when they're plucked
They make a beautiful tune.

Logan Prové (11)
Carterton Community College, Carterton

7KD Sends A Postcard Home

(Inspired by 'A Martian Sends A Postcard Home' by Craig Raine)

Car
Each one has a unique shape and size,
The key opens a portal containing buttons and knobs,
Each one has cushiony spaces for you to gaze at the world,
On each side appears a magical box filled with musical pleasures.

Phone
A minute box with unlimited memory,
Each one has a unique code, which has to be shared to use it,
Each one has a different melody,
Every day a different face.

Door
A black hole that sucks up the impossible
A flat portal leading to another dimension,
Never to see the person who walked through again,
It opens and closes automatically or by hand,
To shut out the never-ending darkness.

Computer
A window leading to the world, which is known as WWW.
A stretched pad with several buttons with different symbols,
An egg which controls a pointer on the window.

Zoe Haydon (11)
Carterton Community College, Carterton

7KD Sends A Postcard Home

(Inspired by 'A Martian Sends A Postcard Home' by Craig Raine)

A minute box with an unlimited memory,
Each one has a unique code, which has to be
Shared to use it.
Each one has a different melody
Every day a different face.

Humans are obsessed with this greasy stuff!
We see them non-stop eating,
On this planet we see some die because of it,
Hot or cold, yucky or nice, it may even run away.

Humans scream when they're on this,
There's a thrill round every corner,
On this planet we see some cry because of its ups and downs,
Lefts and rights, round and splash,
They may even go on again.

Humans always cry when they get there,
There's something wrong with them.
Then they go into rooms
With knives and bloodsuckers and people,
Gowns and hats,
I'm not sure why.

Libby Exley (11)
Carterton Community College, Carterton

Artwork

A way with the magic pen
R ub out again and again
T oning up my work, making it better
W orking away, sketching up to the last minute
O utside thinking what to draw next
R ubbing out again
K eep up the good work.

Natasha Rudge (12)
Carterton Community College, Carterton

7KD Sends A Postcard Home

(Inspired by 'A Martian Sends A Postcard Home' by Craig Raine)

A minute box with an unlimited memory,
Each one has a unique code, which has to be shared to use it,
Each one has a different melody,
Every day a different face.

A black hole that sucks up the impossible,
A flat portal leading to another dimension,
Never to see the person who walked through again,
It opens and closes automatically or by hand,
To shut out the never-ending darkness.

You stuff your ears with plastic balls
Which connect to a small box,
Thin strips attach to both
And when you turn it on
Boom, boom! into your ears!

It lights up the corner of the room,
It brings news, entertainment and information
Into the home at the touch of a button,
Some say it will make your eyes go square
If you stare at it for too long!

Henry Stephens [11]
Carterton Community College, Carterton

Christmas Morning

As I wake to a wondrous, white world,
A chill straight down my spine,
From a frosty snowflake.

As I step out into the garden,
I feel the deep, white snow
Crunch under my feet,
Like some sort of everlasting dream.

Thomas Dickinson [14]
Carterton Community College, Carterton

I Will Put In My Box

(Inspired by 'Magic Box' by Kit Wright)

I will put in my box . . .
The sound of a mythical saxophone,
The amazing touch of my parents' arms around me,
The sport I like, running around the track,
The fuzzy feeling of me falling down.

I will put in my box . . .
Having my parties, sleepovers too,
Games I will play forever on end,
Watching TV on my own,
Getting excited on Christmas Day,
Opening presents minute after minute,
Throwing paper everywhere.

I will put in my box . . .
The food I love, curries and chicken,
Eating away at chicken everyday,
Getting pudding twice a week,
Going to my lovely bed,
Where I can relax.

This is what I put in my box!

Rebecca Sanderson (12)
Carterton Community College, Carterton

Birthday

B undles of joy,
   waiting to be released into the world
I nternal rage flowing through your veins,
   pleading with you to open your presents
R umble as a snowball hits the side of the house wall.
   Crash!
T eams stacked against you, the race is on,
   who will make the biggest snowman?
H unger and passion is shown,
   determination is proven
D anger, as tensions build, joy and harmony plummet down -
   war cries are shouted, it suddenly is a free for all
A lmost at the end of the day,
   starting to huff and puff
Y ou're at the end of the day, you can finally release new life
   into the world. You decide . . .

      Bundles of joy
                  Presents
      New Life.

Dylan Moyce (12)
Carterton Community College, Carterton

The Time Of The Samurai

Time is life
But not just one
Speedy, like the glaze of the knife
But anything would put up a fight
With the moon as its guide
It's never afraid to hide
When the moonlit stars shine on
The forest creatures gaze in fear
Something to seek when darkness falls
Knowing then they leave their homes
They might not come back alive
Gems and jewels
Beautiful as the swipe of his sword
He leads a dangerous life
The breeze of summer days they go alone
But when the moon comes up
They fight as one
In the time of the Samurai!

Chloe King (12)
Carterton Community College, Carterton

Molly

'Dad, Dad, we must be nearly there!'
Feeling to excited, can't stop smiling.
Dad looks round, scruffing up his hair
Which he spent ages styling.
Next thing I know we're outside her door,
We knock, we wait, she comes,
'All those puppies,' she said, 'there's more and more!'
We smile, her house smells like freshly baked buns.
Small and innocent her cute little face,
I wanted to take her home,
Out of this place!

Megan Pearson (13)
Carterton Community College, Carterton

Rough Times In The War

The war is a dangerous place to be
Nothing is about me, me, me
I try my hardest to stay alive
Thinking of my family, I need to survive

Running across the hot, muddy grounds
All I can hear are really loud sounds
The guns are all firing everywhere I go
But they told me to just 'go with the flow'

Wearing my body armour when it is so hot
I can't take it off as I could get shot
My helmet is for safety as it protects my head
I have to keep thinking positively or I could be dead

Returning to the camp for a well-earned rest
The feeling of my body armour from off my chest
I lie in my bed where I wish I could stay
But I'm up in six hours to fight another day.

Aimee Felstead (13)
Carterton Community College, Carterton

Harry, The Dog

H appy as ever, Harry gets excited when I come down after
    I've woken up
A fter my breakfast I get dressed and
    we go off for a walk
R un, run, he goes along the grass,
    stopping every so often to sniff

R olling on the grass, having a good time
    with grass stains on his ears and nose
Y elling him to come back, he runs like mad
    back at home he flops on his bed, fast asleep.
    My dog, Harry.

Chloe Wingrove (13)
Carterton Community College, Carterton

Alysia Sends A Postcard Home

(Inspired by 'A Martian Sends A Postcard Home' by Craig Raine)

A minute box with an unlimited memory,
That has a unique code, which has to be shared to use it,
They all have a different melody,
Every day a different face.
A passageway, full of excitement,
Bursting with colour,
Every button you press
Is packed full of more and more dimensions,
Its reflective surface opens the door to a new world,
Each one has a different shape and size.
The key opens the portal door,
Containing lots of little buttons.
Everyone has a cushiony space
For you to gaze out on the world.
On each side appears a magical box,
Filled with musical pleasures.

Alysia Anderton (11)
Carterton Community College, Carterton

Will I

Will I die today? Go, just like that?
Will I fight today? Shoot anyone dead?
Will there be an IED today?
Blow anyone up?
Will I lose a colleague today?
Will they just go?

Will the war end today?
Will it just be another day?
Will I?
Will it?
    Will it always be the question?

Sophie Brain (13)
Carterton Community College, Carterton

I Am Slavery

I am starvation
I am blood
I am the chains that tie you up

I am death
I am hate
I am your silence, your nightmare, your fate

I am grief
I am a prison
I am your master, listen, just listen!

An enemy
A foe
An opponent
A rival

I am slavery . . .

Ellen Moore [14]
Carterton Community College, Carterton

Memories From The Beach

The smell of the ocean and the seaweed floating,
The water rushing and hitting children's feet
As they jump the waves.
The crunch of shells under your feet
As you run across the scorching sand.
The tap, tap, tapping of people playing
Bat and ball on the shore.
The icy cold seawater touching your sun-baked skin
As you go for a swim.
The excited squeals of happy children
Running and playing on the beach.
The rippling of kites in the wind above you,
The refreshing, cold taste of ice cream in your mouth.

Bethan Milner [12]
Carterton Community College, Carterton

Love

Happiness is love,
They start as a mate,
Sent from above
Turns into a date.

People can engrave
What they want to say,
My life and heart will never cave,
He always brightens my day.

It's hard to be apart,
Every time I see him smile
It kind of breaks my heart,
It's like a pattern of love on a tile.

Things could change along the way
But to be honest no one can say.

Chloe Wiblin (13)
Carterton Community College, Carterton

Be Good My Son

I hate goodbyes,
I hate hellos,
I hate sad lies,
I hate the blows.

I'm waiting here,
I'm waiting there,
The people I knew,
The love we share.

But now it's time,
My deeds are done,
I won't return,
Be good, my son.

Amber Exley (13)
Carterton Community College, Carterton

That One Puppy

Both of us too excited to speak,
Only the sound of cars rushing past.
The dull, red apple skin cold against my own,
Scenery of trees and fields flashed by.
The young puppy, confused as she looked out,
Little barks of happiness and sadness.
She laid her head and front paws on my lap
And gently licked my trouser leg.
That small puppy face, looking up at me,
With big, brown eyes staring.
We tried so many names,
But eventually we came up with Maya.
I called, 'Maya,' she looked up,
So that was that,
The one puppy, Maya.

Tierney Kelman [11]
Carterton Community College, Carterton

Book

Eye-catching front cover,
Disturbing your eyes in a pleasant way,
Revealing the story's secret.
Trapped words inside the locked book
That's waiting to be opened.
Filled with unread words
That shortly will fascinate your mind.

Pages hidden in dramatic sentences,
Behind each page there's a different part to the story,
Telling you the unexpected.

All the magic, romance and drama,
Keeping your mind busy and eyes focused.

Vicky Bakula [12]
Carterton Community College, Carterton

7KD Sends A Postcard Home

(Inspired by 'A Martian Sends A Postcard Home' by Craig Raine)

A minute box with an unlimited memory,
Each one has a unique code, which has to be shared to use it,
Each one has a different melody,
Every day a different face.

The bowl of misery all on its own,
Relieves you from your discomfort,
Down the waterslide it goes,
When you visit you lock yourself in.

She looks over the country,
Like a tiger after its prey,
Wherever she goes everyone respects her,
She's ruled over England for 60 years
And nobody can change that.

Lucy Grisman & Lois Smith
Carterton Community College, Carterton

The Soldier

I am courage
I am brave
I am bold
I am death

I am friendship
I am ready
I am angry
I am emotion

I am fear
I am scared
I am strong
I am the soldier!

Tom Hurren [13]
Carterton Community College, Carterton

The Front Line

I remember the gunshots,
The fear one might hit me,
Thinking, will I ever see my family again?
My kids, my parents and even my dogs.

I would miss them all dearly,
All I could think of were the times I spent with them.
I knew one mistake, one wrong movement,
I could be dead,
Knowing any minute my head
Could be blown right off.

Laying there, with the adrenaline running,
Your heart pumping faster than ever,
But knowing that you were fighting for your country,
Knowing, one day, you might be renowned as a hero.

Liam Morris (13)
Carterton Community College, Carterton

War

I am the fire that never goes out
I am the blood that is shed
I am the bullets that are wasted
I am the lives that are lost
I am never-ending
I am war!

I am the poppies that grow so slowly
I am the towns and cities that were bombed
I am never-ending
I am war!

Torin Harley (13)
Carterton Community College, Carterton

It's Getting Chilly In Chile

Crash, crash!
Go the rocks in Chile.
Crash, bang!
Go the shovels in Chile.
Crash, rustle!
Go the miners in Chile.
Crash, thud!
I think it's getting chilly in Chile!

Rustle, rustle!
Go the survivors in Chile.
Rustle, groan!
Go the miners in Chile.
Rustle, questions!
Go the wonders in Chile.
Rustle, scream!
I think that it's getting chilly in Chile.

Sighs, silence!
Goes the patience of Chile.
Sighs, drills!
Go the rescuers in Chile.
Sighs, cries!
Go the families in Chile.
Sighs, gasps!
I think it's getting chilly in Chile.

Cheers, cheers!
Go the people of Chile.
Cheers, screeches!
Goes the capsule of Chile.
Cheers, chants!
Go the campers of Chile.
Cheers, cries!
Maybe it's not getting chilly in Chile after all!

Crash, crash!
Go the rocks in Chile.
Crash, bang!
Go the shovels in Chile.
Crash, rustle!
Go the miners in Chile.
Crash, thud!
That was the chill in Chile!

Charmaine Smethurst (10)
Etonbury Middle School, Arlesey

A Crow

I'll let you know
That as a crow,
A very pretty bird,
I am so black,
With more impact,
I cannot fly too low.

The best part is,
When in a tizz,
My wings just flap and flap,
I cannot help
But love myself,
As I can trust dear Liz.

So, to conclude,
My favourite mood
Has to be temptation,
For when I see
A shiny thing,
It's like a tempting food.

Talena Day (12)
Etonbury Middle School, Arlesey

What Matters To Me?

What matters to me?
Seeing the sun shining.

What matters to me?
The rainforest and mining.

What matters to me?
Penguins and global warming.

What matters to me?
Arguments and no warnings.

What matters to me?
My family and friends.

What matters to me?
Tying up loose ends.

What matters to me?
Watching the grass grow.

What matters to me?
The cold winter and snow.

What matters to me?
To do what I want to do.

What matters to me?
What matters to you?

Ella Burns (11)
Etonbury Middle School, Arlesey

A Winter Poem

Winter, winter, here it comes.
Winter, winter, it's so much fun.
Winter, winter, here it comes,
Get ready for winter everyone.

Kayleigh Little (10)
Etonbury Middle School, Arlesey

Friendship

Friendship
It takes more than caring
To be a real friend,
The nature of friendship
Requires a blend
Of warmest compassion

Love
Someone to be true to us,
Whether near or apart,
Someone whose love
We'll always hold in out heart.

Last loved friend
Make new friends
But keep the old,
One is silver
The other gold.

Love is to be cherished.

Dylan Joseph (13)
Etonbury Middle School, Arlesey

Simple Summer Breeze

The thing I love most about a simple summer breeze
Is hearing the repeating sound of the little honeybees
But sometimes the pollen makes my little nose sneeze
However, I would rather sneeze than smell mouldy cheese
As I turn on my sunbed, in my pocket I hear the jingling of keys
As I do this, I think, at ease
How much I love the simple summer breeze.

Alice Page (12)
Etonbury Middle School, Arlesey

Summer's Nearly Here

Summer's nearly here,
Grandad steers me near,
To the place I love the most,
On the sunny Bournemouth coast,
Summer's nearly here.

Strawberry, chocolate and vanilla ice cream,
All those swimmers are so keen,
The big waves thrashing and crashing,
Summer's nearly here.

Oh, those surfers, riding the waves,
People exploring in the caves,
Lots of sand
Covering lots of land,
Summer's nearly here.

So jump in the car,
It's really not far,
Summer's nearly here.

Emma Boughton (11)
Etonbury Middle School, Arlesey

What Matters To Me

What matters to me?
Do you know?
Is it warmth or is it snow?
Do I care about the world
Or am I just a selfish girl?
Do I love my family
Or do I care just about me?
Do I call this town my home,
Or is it just my house alone?
Do my gadgets really matter
Or are they just junk and dusty clutter?
Furry Uggs and lovely clothes,
Are they important?
I don't know.

Rhiannon Mackie (12)
Etonbury Middle School, Arlesey

A Couple Of Things That Matter To Me

What matters to me,
What matters to me
Is my friends and family.

What matters to me,
What matters to me,
The key in life is to be happy.

What matters to me,
What matters to me
Might not matter to you.

What matters to me,
Well what can I say?
All the good things in life are free.

Niamh Coughlan (11)
Etonbury Middle School, Arlesey

Season Poem

When leaves have fallen
And harvest is near,
I wonder how long till Christmas is here.

Now the snow has landed
And Christmas is near,
I realise it's near the end of the year.

The flowers have blossomed,
Now the birds are singing,
Animals and insects hibernating.

The summer holidays have started,
I'm ready for the pool,
I've started dreading the time to go back to school.

Maya Dhaliwal (11)
Etonbury Middle School, Arlesey

Take Wing

I will walk with you to the waterfall,
I can't turn my back,
You can't answer my call.

You'll follow me until times demise,
To world's end or the death of my mind.

You're that wandering cry,
Tricked by a lullaby,
I'm the endless desert
Full of murmurs and sighs.

You're the one who returned,
In body you're mine.
I'm the eternal darkness,
Where you spend your time.

Let me take her home,
I'm begging you,
I'll play a song
So it softens you.

A tune so swift it melts the heart,
Turning your back as the lovers part,
Two more steps and you're free of your fears,
Glance behind as she disappears.

James Anthony Traylen (14)
Farnham Heath End School, Farnham

All About Sports

S port is fun to play
P eople watch through glass
O ranges, which people have at half-time
R ugby is fast
T ennis makes a whooshing noise.

William Moffett (14)
Fitzwaryn School, Wantage

The Future

The future is exciting
Because it makes me independent
The future is scary
Because you have to go to college
The future makes me nervous
Because I have to train to be a hairdresser
The future makes me pleased
Because the future will give you advice
The future is
For everybody and never-ending.

Chantell Moffatt (15)
Fitzwaryn School, Wantage

Winter

Winter is freezing air,
If you step on the snow it makes a crunching sound.
The snow is white,
If you go outside you should wear warm clothing.
If you pick the snow up, it is soft.
When it is hot the snow melts.
When the snow melts and you step on it. It sounds squidgy.
When it is completely melted, it's wet.

Brett Hemingway (15)
Fitzwaryn School, Wantage

Sea

The sea is very beautiful,
The sea is blue and green,
The sea has lots of seaweed and whales
And fish and crabs and dolphins.
So why are people lazy?
They should put rubbish in the bin,
It could make lots of fish die.
Pollution is bad, recycling is good.
Why don't people listen?
The sea is very beautiful,
The see is blue and green,
I like to see it clean.

Lorna Freestone [13]
Gosden House School, Guildford

Tunnelling, Tumbling And Talking

Two long tails, four sparkling eyes,
Tunnelling, squeaking and jumping to surprise.
Tumbling over each other, from fight or play,
Two gerbils together, named Sweet and Spicy.
Tunnelling Sweet, watch him go,
Tumbling towards him it's Spicy, oh no!
Talking all night, playing all day,
Two squeaking to the telephone, especially on Sunday.
Tall gerbil, Spicy, so brown, like mud,
Tiptoeing gerbil, Sweet, so white, like ice.
To me my gerbils are more than just nice!

Jessica Short [13]
Gosden House School, Guildford

My Fantastic Dog

My dog is fantastic in lots of ways
He likes his food when I give it to him
My dog really likes his walks
On really hot days he needs lots of water
I go for a walk with my dog every day
I feed him every day because he gets hungry
He likes playing with other dogs
I am always nice to my dog
My dog matters to me
Because he makes me happy.

Hannah Kemp (13)
Gosden House School, Guildford

Animals Matter

I think animals are lovely,
Every animal in our world,
Not everybody thinks so,
Some people have animals,
They don't treat them well,
It makes me sad and cross.

People who love animals
Give lots of love and care
That makes me feel great.

Katarina Feroce (13)
Gosden House School, Guildford

44

Let Them Live

I love all the animals I see in my country, Zimbabwe,
Long nosed, big ears and gentle elephants.
People kill them for money, I feel very upset that they do that.
Simply white and black, staying in a group.
Zebras should be free, snakes do sometime bite.
But they still need to live.
Chimpanzees, gorillas.
I should always be able to see the animals
And so should all my kids.

Yeukai Kamoto [13]
Gosden House School, Guildford

Forever And Always

The best thing for me
Is going to see
My Farncombe mates.
We muck about in a funny way
And joke around all day.
We laugh and laugh and laugh
We stick up for each other too.
Mates are really important to me
And that's what matters to me.

Courtney Chedd [13]
Gosden House School, Guildford

My Family Are Fun

M y family are lovely
Y es, I love them all

F un, exciting, happy house
A special day today
M y birthday
I am thirteen
L ots of food and presents
Y ou should see my smile.

Rachel Livingstone (13)
Gosden House School, Guildford

Pieces Of Me

The pieces of me are everywhere really
This piece is laid against that tired oak, where we once lay
Its figure a mere shadow as you approach
Day by day
Year by year
My piece does not change, but gathers with fear
Your piece is different
The roots of that familiar oak bind strong
But my piece weakens at the sight of your smile; so delicate . . .

My piece cowers as your footsteps brush past,
Leaving a trail of emptiness, to Hell
You move forward without thought or hesitation
You do not even glance at the sight of the past
Yet my piece is frozen
Frozen to the memories of what once was
Unable to break free

There are many pieces of me
Yet not all are for you to see.

Joe McQuilken (16)
Havant College, Havant

My Last Birthday

The work, the study and evolution of time
is a theory that's still in the depth of its prime,
Because the eggheads and boffins still can't figure out
why time is a concept we can't live without.
Who really cares is time moves so fast,
When new generations destroy things of past?
While memories of loved ones become dashed and plain -
I see no more sunlight, nor the stir of rain.
I see no more summers and no more springs,
Only the discomfort that time will bring.
The painful awareness that time's no good;
washing over the place where friends once stood.
Degrading our lives or just thieving them away.
Who knows who'll see their last birthday?
At last, there's just me - left all alone, wind in my hair,
I hear a strange moan,
This incessant moan, time and again,
begging the question of my determined end.
And yet more time passes, one last birthday is here
and never so swift has time flown in a year.
I've lived a full life, for that I am proud, but now my time is calling loud.
So as night submerges me and the day has moved on,
I blow out my candles and wish myself gone.

Tom Pickard (16)
Havant College, Havant

The Kind Of Silence

the kind of silence that lingers with the sights of sun
on the soft horizon,
morning, faintly broken by the birds of brilliant choir
(almost, hush, now)
and your lover's lips are locked to your neck in sweet prayer.

the kind of silence that leaves you breathless,
gaps within your chest of empty bubbles floating outwards
from your lungs to leave you partly empty, wondering
(wandering) what could ever happen in this kind of silence.

the kind of silence whose gentle touches maim the thread of your
existence ever so slightly,
stomping bloody footprints all over the face of life and love
alone in the world when it's silent (regardless of silence)
and no one is around to hear the sound of this silence.

the kind of silence when you can't hear anything other than laughter in your
ears,
(ah, to be alive)
cracks of breaths between your teeth and tongue,
almighty speech controlled and this may be your favourite kind of silence.

the kind of silence you don't understand.
the one who bites the bullet you shoot in its face.
the silence who is all but silence
(secrets) and ghosts stand by your bed - whisper.

it's high time you picked a silence, took it from its endless cadence
(choose before you break its violence, bleed it out if all its radiance).

the kind of silence with its padded feet running,
tapping, mostly, on slimy garden grass,
dragging a long stick behind it and smiling
'til kingdom come.

the kind of silence that won't ever let go of your hand
in the dark when your fast heart beats and tells you that's it's all okay,
it's all going to be alright, you only have to wait until the morning's
light and the shadows will fade away: the silence shall stay.

this kind of silence won't ever leave you grip you seize you, take
you under the seas of its breast this kind of silence knows you

best will do your things when you need rest
the rest of the world
knows of this silence you're not alone when the whole world
is silence
and this kind of
silence
is
existence.

the kind of silence you favour
is the silence you choose
to hear for the remainder of your days
as you learn that
every living creature dies alone

and silent.

Nadia Evering [17]
Havant College, Havant

What If

What if I didn't care
For careful quotations
For spelling corrections
For grammar standard?
What if I never cared
For all these principles
For all these barriers?
Would you understand
My own alphabets
My own capitals
And my own full stops?
Or would you 'correct' me?
Or you'll call me nonsense
Or perhaps you do not care
Like I do to yours?

Maza Kebede [16]
Havant College, Havant

Love's Hate

(Dedicated to Jacob Coates)

At night you sleep, I stay awake,
my eyes stretched wide, made no mistake.
I lie and think, is this thing real?
Is this how he should make me feel?
Should I stay? Or should I leave?
He makes me feel so damned naïve.
The early hours, I pack my things,
no clothes, perfume or diamond rings.
He's not for me, I'm just his tool -
sneak out the door; oh what a fool!
What if he wakes and sees me going?
Sneaks up behind without me knowing?

It's time to leave, without a doubt,
case in hand I walk straight out.
What would he do? Be angry for sure.
A slap or a punch
Or walk into the door?

Is this right? last chance to stay . . .
He can be nice in his own way.
He says I've no friends, is it true?
No! That's it! With him I'm through!

His eyes are open, I'm in trouble!
He wants a drink, a vodka double.
One drink, two drink, three drink, four.
What should I do? Run out the door?
I make a sprint down the stairs,
hand on my head, left a trail of hairs.
His face turned red and eyes look dead,
One fist, two fists, three fists, four.
And there, I lie motionless on the floor.

It's not his fault - yeah, I'm to blame,
I angered him plenty, I drove him insane.
I wish him the best with someone new
And now I have to bid adieu!

Bella Sanderson (17)
Havant College, Havant

Time

From the bitter pain it inflicted on my heart,
When it stole from me
The people and things I care for,
Time has never truly healed me.

Although much stronger than I am,
Time kills me with its jealousy.
It rules my life, makes it tough
And knows that I've got enough,
But time cares very less.

I pray and ask for mercy and grace,
But time doesn't listen to mankind.
Mightily pushing me towards the end,
Time maintains its pace.

Time is waiting to take me away.
I have cried too much to worry any longer.
It's only the shadow of the sword,
Time will have no more say
Once I have crossed over to immortality!
Time's only doing its duty,
Time will surely miss me one day.

Kaubo Axell Muyembe (17)
Havant College, Havant

A Black Waterfall

Given the way
Her make-up takes
A small part away
From the glow of her face
Sadly, then madly
A black waterfall
A trickle at first
Then the burst
Then the squall.

The forgiveness you seek
Just two black streaks
And when you ask why
There's no alibi for your lie.

Emma Durham (17)
Havant College, Havant

Redemption

(Dedicated to Thomas Pickard)

A golden ray of sunlight glows upon the once brown soil,
And to this country men salute to show that they are loyal.
They drop their arms and dusty vests to look down at their work,
And at a glance, with one great sigh, the darkened clouds berserk.
As shadows draw and conquer land, the sunlight disappears,
And with the rainy battlefield, the water turns to tears.
The tainted ground on which we stood is laundered by our grief,
And as we leave this place unharmed I glance back with belief.
A poppy bud will open in the gentle winds of May,
And with it grows a brand new life, where once my body lay.

Tom Crease (17)
Havant College, Havant

Home

My home's my place to relax,
My place to think,
My place to play.
My home's my place to draw,
My place to write,
My place to be me.

My home smells of cooking,
It smells of cookies,
It smells of love and food.
My home smells of cherries,
Of pie and flowers,
My home smells of me.

My home looks like a cottage,
A castle or a cave!
It looks like a hut on the beach.
My home looks like happiness,
It looks like hugs and kisses,
It looks like me.

My home feels like love,
Like anger and like joy,
It feels like stone.
My home feels like wool,
Like a cushion or a rug.
Like me . . .

Personal.

Lauryn Jackman (11)
Hemdean House School, Reading

Come And Be Our Guest

Far, far down the road, you'll find my home.
It's rather secluded; a place you wouldn't roam.

It's something different from the other 'nice' houses,
It's eerie and queery
And brimming with louses.

There's the howling of bloodhounds
And the crunching of bones.
People never venture here
Specially on their 'lones'.

You must brace yourself before you enter my pad,
A waft of blood will strike you -
Which is quite bad!

I know what you're thinking,
That family are weird!
They're the sort of family that ought to be feared!

We're all bloodsuckers and
Bloodsucking is what we do best,
So welcome to our home,
Come and be our guest!

Monique Skeete (13)
Hemdean House School, Reading

My Home

My home is a beautiful place,
But it can sometimes be
A crying, hatred place,
A cold, uncomfortable place,
But it is always
A sweet-smelling place,
A loving, caring place,
A warm, comfortable place.

Poppy Moroney (14)
Hemdean House School, Reading

54

My Home

My house is warm,
My house is cosy,
When people look around
They are often very nosy.

I stand in the hallway,
I look around,
It's very messy,
But not a sound.

Everything's fluffy,
Because of my cat,
And in every nook and cranny
You'll find a cricket bat.

My house is warm,
My house is small,
I couldn't fault it,
Not at all!

Ellie Chapman (13)
Hemdean House School, Reading

Home

Home is where the heart is
Smiles are placed
Filled with love and grace
Home is where the heart is.

Home is where the love is
Joy and happiness
Tears and sadness
Home is where the love is.

Charlie Pembroke (11)
Hemdean House School, Reading

Home

A welcoming shout from my cat,
A strong gust of wind tickles me,
A faint smell of scented candles,
As I stand in my entry.

A sound of crashing and chinking,
A draught of steam in addition,
A strong scent of dinner,
As I walk into my kitchen.

A buzz of the television,
An awareness of security,
An aroma of pot-pourri,
As I sit on my settee.

A silence so loud it deafens me,
A feeling of ease,
A tang of perfume,
As I fall asleep.

Phoebe Powell (13)
Hemdean House School, Reading

Home

Home is the place where I can relax,
Home is the place where I play my sax,
Home is the place where I feel cool,
Home is the place where I play in the pool.

Home is the place where I can cook,
Home is the place where I read my book,
Home is the place where I feel secure,
Home is the place where I feel mature.

Corrie Knowles (13)
Hemdean House School, Reading

Are You Still There?

Open and smashed
Taken and gone
Call the police
Nine, nine, nine

Heard a noise
Stepped outside
Ran and ran
Cried and cried

Gate door open
They ran out
Wearing a mask
Scared to death

Where have they gone?
Are they still here?
If you are
Get out and clear!

Stephanie Robinson (12)
Hemdean House School, Reading

My Home

Home is a place of warmth,
For most
A loving, caring, sweet-smelling place.
A comforting, fluffy, sunshiny place.

Home is a place of tears and anger.
For many
Fighting, biting, hating place.
Teary, noisy, full of hatred.

Georgia Doran (13)
Hemdean House School, Reading

Home

The place to go is home . . .
A 'nice to see you' home,
A children exploding home
This is my way home.

A gently touching home,
A hell-hole home,
This-is-the-life home!

A good evening home,
A red with anger home,
This is my dream home.

A tired, but I-won't-go-to-bed home,
A stomping with noise home,
This is my way home . . .

Tilly Wallace (11)
Hemdean House School, Reading

Home

Home is where the heart is,
A warm, gooey marshmallow,
Giving love to any fellow,
A cuddly bear; give me a hug!

It welcomes strangers,
Far and near,
Saying free hugs for everyone here!
Home is where the heart is.

Home is wherever you store your love,
Rooms to store the hatred and greed,
A place that caters for every need,
Home is where your heart is.

Lucy Harris (13)
Hemdean House School, Reading

Home

Light rooms, dark rooms,
Happy rooms, sad rooms,
Cold rooms hot rooms
And even hide and seek rooms.

Viewing rooms, pitch-black rooms,
Tidy rooms, messy rooms,
Quiet rooms, loud rooms
And amazingly enough - daydreaming rooms.

Claustrophobic rooms,
Open rooms, scary rooms,
Excitement rooms, crying rooms,
We have them all!

Safiya Hussain [12]
Hemdean House School, Reading

My Home

My home loves me,
Its warmth envelops me,
Blocking out all the bad feelings,
Making me feel carefree.

My home loves me,
Smells of cooking,
Saunter round the house,
Tummies rumble, mouths' water.

My home loves me,
Especially my room,
My duvet wraps me with
Hugs, love and happiness.

Sophie Harris [13]
Hemdean House School, Reading

The Wounded Man

Wet and windy on the moors
The moon sailing across the clouds,
Like a ghost, sinister, lonely,
Yet, somehow, beautiful.

The wind rustles the grass,
Across the hills the wind moans
Like a wounded man, lonely,
In pain and desperation.

He stumbles through the night,
Looking for shelter,
His feet are blistered, his clothes are ragged,
His eyes are sunken,
His cuts are jagged.

So, if you ever go out to the moor,
Be aware, the wounded man
Is waiting . . .
Waiting . . .
Waiting . . .

His arms open wide in a cold
Embrace from which
He won't relinquish.

Beware
The wounded
Man.

Eve Pearson [13]
Leighton Park School, Reading

Meadows - Haiku

Meadows fluttering
In summer's breeze, butterflies
Elegantly fly.

Greta Kitch [11]
Leighton Park School, Reading

Poverty

Lonely child wants to eat,
With dirty clothes, on a dirty street,
Like a skeleton; skin and bones,
He is hungry, his stomach groans.

Walking back down the lane,
His joints hurting, he's in pain,
And then, when he gets home,
He and his sister all alone.

His mother died when he was three,
His father in a catastrophe,
So he has to clean and cook
And eat the bread that he took.

Working on a plantation in the day,
Him and a friend are led astray,
The owner finds them in a field
And a whip does he yield.

With a smarting hand and back,
A day's pay does he lack,
Going hungry once again,
Will he get food? Where? When?

Max Jennings (12)
Leighton Park School, Reading

Love

Usually when we think of love we think of loving someone
Or a person.
But in my case, love is loving something and not someone.
Love is when you're passionate about something,
Such as music or sport.

So next time you think of loving something or someone,
Think of something you're passionate and care about.

Mahlah Catline (11)
Leighton Park School, Reading

What Matters To Me

I've never been good at much at all, but that's just me,
I'm terrible at chemistry and don't forget PE.
I can't do rugby, football, cricket, believe me this is true,
Volleyball, bowls and rounders, I couldn't throw a shoe.
The periodic table just messes with my mind,
When we cut in biology I sit out to the side.

I can't do RE with those confusing religious cults,
When I'm in DT I always drop the bolts
History is very hard with all those stupid dates.
When I have a French lesson, I end up being late.
Music with me is trouble with all those musical notes,
Don't get me started with those politics,
With their very 'famous' quotes.
But there's something I'm amazing at, I believe with all my heart,
Is English, 'cos let's be honest, English is a laugh.
I'm always getting questioned when our teacher sets us prep,
What can I say, out of everyone I'm definitely the best.
I've never been good at much at all, well I guess that's me,
But English well . . . what can I say, that's my cup of tea!

Finbar Aherne [12]
Leighton Park School, Reading

Pets

I have a dog called Hershey
Named after American Chocolate
He is two and I bet he likes you.

I have a kitty called Snicky
He sleeps all day and night
And sometimes fights with my other cat . . .

Called Welly
His tummy looks like jelly
And he likes to watch the telly.

Gilly Hines [11]
Leighton Park School, Reading

Keeping Me Young

Mud splattered up my bare legs
My trainers pressed the mud from the ground
I could hear him panting as he raced after me
The warm breath against my leg was sharply followed
By a cold, wet nose.
He swerved in front of me, making me fall backwards
Into a quagmire of mud
Joyfully he sprang onto my tummy
In order to completely cover me in mud
I smiled
And in his way he smiled back.

He matters because he keeps my heart young
Even though my body is forcing me to mature
He matters because I love him.

Aimee Fullbrook (14)
Leighton Park School, Reading

Miaow

The miaow is annoying
The miaow is relieving
The miaow is warm
The miaow is cold

The miaow has a bird
The miaow has a rat
The miaow has a mouse
The miaow has a hunger for food

The miaow needs stroking
The miaow needs feeding
The miaow needs excitement
The miaow needs sleep

The miaow is wonderful.

Scott Morgan
Leighton Park School, Reading

Birds

Birds who fly
Way in the sky
So no more
Of them
I can see.

I dream
Of going
With them
My worries
Fly away.

Fly with them
No more of me
Can anyone see.

Emilia Dixon (11)
Leighton Park School, Reading

The Time No Longer Passes By

We've run out of things to say
We're sitting silently in the hay
Waiting for a bit of inspiration
We've been waiting all day.

The last thing we said was
'Oh, look at that butterfly . . .'
And then I started to wonder why
The time no longer passes by.

Victoria Roberts (13)
Leighton Park School, Reading

The Sweet Sound

A clean, sweet stroke, oh what a lovely sound
Rolls towards the target along the ground
Cheers erupt from all around, harshly shattering the sweet sound
One more stroke along the sweet, green grass
The cheers ponder in my head
My arm slid to swing back again towards the ball
It rolls towards the hole, for every metre a mile of tension
Until the cheers don't need to ponder in my head anymore.

Will Likely (12)
Leighton Park School, Reading

Archery

A ccuracy
R ecurve bow
C ompound bow
H it your target
E xhilarating
R eally fun
Y ou do the work.

Ben Pearson (11)
Leighton Park School, Reading

Wembley

W alking a lot
E xciting
M ore seats than you could imagine
B est stadium ever
L ights everywhere
E njoyable
Y ou will love it.

Joe Hadman (11)
Leighton Park School, Reading

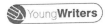

Meerkats

They sit there all day
Licking themselves
Digging tunnels
And making
Cheap
Car comparison websites.

Charlie Hopkinson (13)
Leighton Park School, Reading

They

They are always there.
They know how you feel.
They love you whatever you do.
They are soft bundles of joy.
They are my dogs, Monty and Dougal.

Rawdie Marks (11)
Leighton Park School, Reading

Giraffe

Their necks are long,
They stand up tall,
They reach the trees
And never fall.

Will Lewis (13)
Leighton Park School, Reading

Chocolate -Haiku

Confectionery
Lickable, smooth and tasty
Cadbury or Mars.

Max Parfitt (12)
Leighton Park School, Reading

What's Important To Me

Waiting, waiting
For the moment the Earth falls.
It will someday.
Someday it will burn to a crisp and die.

Waiting, waiting
For the time when the Earth fails.
The Earth will pollute
And everything will be mute.

The parliament will set on fire
And the smoke will rise.
The flags will fall
And the buildings will be no more.

Waiting, waiting
For the moment of screaming.
The time of selfishness
And the cars beeping.

The people will give up,
For there is nowhere to flee,
The news will shut down
And the richest will be the ones who leave.

Waiting, waiting
For the time when love will not be anymore,
If only we could save our home
But someday it will burn to a crisp and fall down.

Jessica Vevers (12)
Luckley Oakfield School, Wokingham

The Character

Behind the mask,
In the play, in which I act
The realist is uncovered,
The optimist is released.

My eyes turn into waterfalls,
When my real face us uncovered
And yet my heart will sink,
When they look at the character.

Not me, will they see,
Not me, will they love.
And not me will they understand.
The character's their ally.

Nor will they see,
That the character's not me,
Surrounded by people.
Yet still, so alone.

But the character's my enemy,
The person whom I hate.
The one I have to beat,
To show the real me.

All I really want,
Is the character to walk away,
To realise that I will win,
Somehow, some day.

Why can't people see,
That I'm not what they believe,
Not what they conceive,
To be the real me.

All my life, I was too weak,
A rabbit caught in the headlights,
The car not looking out for me,
Frozen, waiting for death.

My cheeks, turn crimson,
When someone bothers to see,
The person behind the mask,
The completely real me.

Jessica Arnold
Luckley Oakfield School, Wokingham

A True Friend

They are always there for you,
Troubles to laughs,
Like the beat of your heart,
The smile on your face,
And when you're down they will bring you back up again,

When they hurt,
You hurt,
They add the skip in your step,
They're like the little bounce when you walk with confidence,
And when you're down they will bring you back up again.

When they smile,
You smile,
Like the cute face of a kitten,
They tell you a random joke you don't get one day,
And the next day you burst out laughing
Because you suddenly get it,
And when you're down they will bring you right up again.

When they cry,
You cry,
When you meet your true friend,
You know it's true, they swear to never ever leave you,
Like the face of a puppy, kind and sweet,
We are like the sun and the moon, complete opposites,
Though we match together perfectly,
And when they're down you will bring them right back up again.

That's the sign of a true friend!

Brittany Meakin (12)
Luckley Oakfield School, Wokingham

What Matters To Me

Imagine a pool of dirty water, what would that look like?
It would be slow running, full of dead things.
Green stuff would float on it, foamy scum and dirt.
Some people have to drink that, they have no choice,
They trudge for miles every day
To get to a pool of dirty water
Full of dirt and animal poop,
Then carry it back to their family
For them to drink and to wash in.

Now imagine a jug of pure water,
It's not hard, we see it every day,
We hear it every night,
The steady drip, drip of the water, coming from the tap,
The spray of a hosepipe, one press and the water comes out,
The feel of the rain beating on your face.

For us to swallow sea water is the most disgusting thing to do,
It tastes of salt and seaweed
But for them it tastes of chocolate.

What they would give
To live in the world that we take for granted,
To feel the soft sea spray on their face,
To drink that cold, clear water that runs out of our tap,
They would love to bring fresh water to their families.
How can we sit by and know that this is happening,
These people should be able to have water that they can drink
Without poisoning themselves instead.

Lottiey Boyd
Luckley Oakfield School, Wokingham

What Matters To Me

I am the king of the forest -
But not for long,
Someone is coming,
Something dangerous is coming,
That won't be stopped.

They know what they want
And they always get it,
They show no emotion
Like they don't even care,
And they won't be stopped.

I hear them coming,
I know they are there,
It happened to my mother,
I was but a cub
And they couldn't be stopped.

They want my fur,
For purses and coats,
They think only of money,
They want nothing else
And they won't be stopped.

I take one last breath,
As I hear the gun load,
And the last thing I see,
Were the eyes of the hunter,
As cold as ice.

Ellie Angus (12)
Luckley Oakfield School, Wokingham

The Hurt

The wind is a scream for mercy
Haunting the forests at night
Drought is sent to warn us
Of the venom in our bite
The hurt eyes of the Earth gaze into the stars
And cry into the shoulders of Venus and Mars.

Floods are the tears of anguish
Washing away our cold lives
Crystal snow soothes weeping wounds
Carved by our brutal knives
The hurt eyes of the Earth gaze into the stars
And cry into the shoulders of Venus and Mars.

Clouds are soft blankets of sorrow
Hiding scars from fiery eyes
Earthquakes smash the spine of hate
The stifles our home's sighs
The hurt eyes of the Earth gaze into the stars
And cry into the shoulders of Venus and Mars.

How cruel is the human conscience
Letting us twist how it seems
How cruel is the human mind
Letting us block the screams
The hurt eyes of the Earth gaze into the stars
And cry into the shoulders of Venus and Mars.

Amy Martin (12)
Luckley Oakfield School, Wokingham

Matters To Me

These are the things that matter to me.

The dew on the grass, the clouds in the sky
To hear the tune of the birds nearby
They flutter to my window to sing with all their might
They put me to bed in the cold, winter's night.

These are the things that matter to me.

The smile on the faces that matter to me
The joy, the laughter, like the buzz of a bee
The voice of happiness fills the room
When we see the return of the bride and groom.

These are the things that matter to me.

They run, they run, run for their lives
For the brutal hunters are speeding by.
The click of the ammo pushed down the gun
The echo in the valley since it is done.

These are the things that matter to me.

Upon the walls are the stuffed little creatures
To some look nice as one of the features
The eyes wide open, no not a blink
They shine and glisten, they're dark as black ink.

These are the things that matter to me.

Milly Golightly [12]
Luckley Oakfield School, Wokingham

Friends

One day I was lonely,
One day I was sad,
One day I had nowhere to go,
I stood out from the crowd.

One day someone came along,
She talked to me,
Made me feel wanted,
And liked me for who I was.

This was called a friend,
Friends matter most to me,
They are the sun, moon and stars.

They are sometimes icy like frost,
Other times they are warm like the sun,
Like a flower they grow.

My best friend is like a diary,
I can tell her anything
And she will listen,
She won't let anyone open her and read her.

But I can read her like a diary,
I'm the one with the golden key.

Sophie Bryson (12)
Luckley Oakfield School, Wokingham

What Matters To Me?

What if the Earth splits,
and keeps falling down and down.
And the world's face is nothing but a frown.
That's what matters to me.

Wondering when the Earth shrinks,
shrivelling down to a tiny pea size.
And on planet Mars it lies.
That's what matters to me.

What if the Earth catches on fire,
there's no water to hose it down.
So the Queen can never more wear her darling crown.
That's what matters to me.

Wondering when the Earth freezes,
where everywhere there's frost.
And all lives are lost.
That's what matters to me.

What if the Earth just dies,
what happens to me?
What happens to you?

That's what happens to me.

Minami Ishii
Luckley Oakfield School, Wokingham

What Matters To Me

I am the lifesaver,
I help the thirsty,
Save them from destruction.

I am the life bringer,
Life would not exist without me,
I am the secret elixir from which life was born.

But I might not be for long,
My time is coming to an end
If you don't stop the destruction of me.

You are the water stopper,
Polluting my lungs until I can't breathe

But . . .

You could be the water saver,
And save me from destruction.

You could be the water bringer,
Bringing me to the desperate.

If you don't follow my advice,
Your time might be coming to an end
And I can't stop the destruction of you.

Catherine Tren (12)
Luckley Oakfield School, Wokingham

What Matters To Me?

What matters to me?
My parents and my family,
My grandma who is old and ill,
Great Aunty Bet who lives alone,
My cousin who is getting married.

Stopping global warming is best,
Our world is in distress,
The wars that rage on and on,
Killing both the old and young,
Starvation and hunger for some.

Animal cruelty must be stopped,
Hurting those who can't fight back
Is a senseless act,
Protect endangered species,
Their loss is our loss.

Killing Mother Nature's beauty,
Causing black holes in her forest heart,
Raging fury across her land,
When you feel the earth shudder,
Our world will come apart.

Aleanor Bakes [12]
Luckley Oakfield School, Wokingham

The Things That Matter To Me

The things that matter to me is seeing my dog Noodle after school,
Him leaping up at me, wagging his tail like he hasn't seen me for days,
Playing outside with him, watching him bark at squirrels and cats.

The things that matter to me is seeing all my friends after the summer holidays,
Talking and listening to them, trusting in them, telling them secrets,
Spending time with them every second of the day.

The things that matter to me is a family occasion,
All of us getting together, sharing good news of what has happened,
Celebrating great things, big or small.

The things that matter to me is nature,
Where would we be without nature, it gets us through life,
It is so beautiful, when the nature goes what happens to us?

The things that matter to me is the world,
The bees are dying out, they're the ones that keep the nature and world alive,
When the bees go what happens to us?

These are the things that matter to me.

Claudia Hughes (13)
Luckley Oakfield School, Wokingham

What Matters To Me

What matters to me is a world which is just and fair,
Where no one lives in fear, pain or hunger,
Where people care for one another.

What matters to me is to live on a planet
Where nature hasn't been torn apart.

Where life, so precious
Can be lived to the full by all.

Gaia Webb (12)
Luckley Oakfield School, Wokingham

What Matters To Me

When the trees shake as if in the middle of a hurricane,
And all the birds fly in lots of different directions,
As long as they are safe,
That's what matters to me.

When the squirrels scramble away like danger is coming,
And all the leaves jumping off the trees,
As long as they are safe,
That's what matters to me.

When the ants flee away like everything is after them,
And when the bushes fight back,
As long as they are safe,
That's what matters to me.

When all goes wrong,
There is no going back,
The fire is burning under
And above us,
Now they are not safe,
I am now running.

Lily Andrews (12)
Luckley Oakfield School, Wokingham

My Pony

My pony is my best friend.
He always knows what I am thinking.
He always cheers me up when I am sad.

He is as bright as the sun
And is as fast as lightning.
He's as soft as velvet.

He's as strong as an elephant
But is as skinny as a stick.
I love my pony to bits.

Safiah Fraser (12)
Luckley Oakfield School, Wokingham

Dirty Water

I'm thirsty, I'm hungry, I need somewhere to stay.
If only I could find a stream to help it go away.
I walk, I run, I try to get away
But somewhere deep inside me, it's settling down to stay.
But then I see it, not too far away
So I run and run until I've gone the way.
And look into it, all shallow, brown and grey.
I drink it up until it's all gone
And settle down for a night without a run.
I wake up; I see the shining bright light,
But somehow it's impossible to lift myself up.
I try, I try I really do,
I shout and cry but nobody's in view.
I think to myself what's happened to me?
And then I realise, it suddenly hits me.
The water, the water I'd been searching for,
With brown and grey and dirt and dust,
It had made me weak, weaker than I must.

Emily Clayton
Luckley Oakfield School, Wokingham

What Matters To Me

What matters to me is when the world dies
And slowly dissolves into darkness.
Exhaust fumes kill the ozone,
Water evaporates into air.
The wind brushing against my face feels cold and deadly.

What matters to me is when the world dies
And the leaves are alive with fire
The sun disintegrates and falls down to Earth
And animals become extinct
No more people, no more life.

Sofia Burchell (12)
Luckley Oakfield School, Wokingham

My Heart Matters To Me

My heart matters to me,
Inside it holds a lot of things,
Love, happiness and life,
When a heart is broken, it is not at all easy to fix,
You can search the world for years on end
To find the right person, the right cure,
In my heart there can be a lot of sorrow,
There can be pain and weakness,
But that is enough about pain and breaking,
There are beautiful parts of the heart,
They are mainly found when you have something called love,
Love can be wicked to a heart
And at the same time can be the most powerful thing in it,
You see without a heart,
We would be just pure stone,
That's why my heart matters to me.

Lucie Smith [12]
Luckley Oakfield School, Wokingham

My Kittens

I have two kittens, they are the best,
But they can be such pests.
They charge around night and day,
Always begging me to play.
On the sofas, on the chairs,
Scratching, clawing lots of tears.
Up the curtains, there they go,
Here comes Mum, oh no . . .
Bounding, running, lots of fun,
Better get out the way,
Here they come!
But my kittens are so sweet,
Especially when they're asleep!
Soft silk fur and velvet paws,
A little pink nose
But very sharp claws!

Scarlett Markham (12)
Luckley Oakfield School, Wokingham

What Matters To Me

She is a fool,
She is a sucker.
My friend had a big lie to me,
For five years.
What matters to me.

I heard my best friend whispering like a devil,
It doesn't really matter,
'I don't really care about her,'
They said.

But still, they don't tell the truth to me.
They betrayed me.
What matters to me.

But still I go to school every day
Like a civil war.

May Sako [13]
Luckley Oakfield School, Wokingham

Tramp

The queue was long
I stood there for ages
Behind me I heard
The rustling of pages
A frail old man holding
Bags filled with junk
Was reading the papers
Of rubbish he stunk
His beanie was stretched
It covered his hair
Itching his beard
People started to stare
Middle-aged gossipers
Shuffled their bags
They spoke of his clothes
He could barely afford rags
Parents told children
Look at that creep
If you mess up at school
You'll be out on the streets
The queue reduced
Once I got served
I waited outside
Like a bundle of nerves
The old man hobbled out
Heavy bags in his arms
I began to approach him
He looked quite alarmed
Excuse me I said
Would you like a hand?
Get lost!
He spat
I could not understand

The tramp limped off
As I wandered alone
Disappointed yet glad
At least I had a home.

Asha Khatun (16)
Luton Sixth Form College, Luton

Sacrifices (War)

Hearts cried
Hearts died
Hearts sacrificed
Shouting, screaming for help
Running over decayed bodies
'Help!' they shouted
Wishing something sprouted
To save them from this nightmare
'Please someone, care!'
They repeated
No one there
Everyone cheated
What did the children do?
What did all the innocent people do?
What did the nation do?
All trees demolished
No more buds . . .

Only floods.

Arooj Javaid Khan Lodhi (16)
Luton Sixth Form College, Luton

Alone

She walks alone,
Down endless corridors of gloom,
She's choking, suffocating,
A life of abnormality,
But of complete reality.

She hides alone,
Hiding feelings, dodging shadows,
Oblivious to the good,
Victim of the bad,
A life misunderstood,
But indeniably sad.

She worries alone,
So as not to drag,
Her friends into this darkness,
Hard to understand but
A life of hate and spite,
Will one day, turn out right.

She sits alone,
As tears spill over,
Pretending everything's fine,
And though she knows,
She's anything but fine,
She keeps quiet, so it doesn't show.

She thinks alone,
Her face changing, contemplating,
Absorbing things around her,
Everything but the good,
No colours, just black and grey emotions.

But she doesn't stay alone,
For I am beside her,
When she needs me,
I am there, listening,
And when she doesn't,
She's happy.

Katie Downer (14)
Mayfield Secondary School, Portsmouth

The Fox

Misunderstood, he lies in wait
For the barks to pass.
The pounding hooves up on the earth,
The dry dust in the air.

They fade away into light,
The little terrors following.
He slinks away into the fields,
Hoping the grass will conceal.

Then the sound of fearsome growls,
A howling that chills to the bone.
The thundering thuds do return,
He stops in his fright.

Then the muscles start to work,
Propelling him forward on unsteady legs.
He is tired, lost, hurting,
Still he runs at breakneck speeds.

But then, with a bang, he does halt,
And slowly to the ground he falls.
His leg lies limp upon the grass,
Crimson rivers through bending green peaks.

The pounding suddenly ceases
But he does not give up quite yet.
With an agonising yelp, he rises up,
Clamps his jaw around his tormentor's leg.

The screams of pain are shrill and harsh
And he waits for the retaliation.
The person reaches for his waist
And produces something sharp and shiny.

To his throat it is held,
Freedom slowly escaping,
And as his orange fur darkens and dampens
He closes his eyes into the realms of never waking.

Jessica Lyn Bonsall (14)
Mayfield Secondary School, Portsmouth

Secret Agent

I am a secret agent
My name is James Bond
My number's 007
And I never get things wrong.

I kill a few people here and there
I hear their screams as I shoot
I've got a gun I carry around
And a dead body in my boot.

I drive an expensive car around
I kiss the girls all day
My favourite place is the Bahamas
That's where I sleep the nights away.

Will I ever get shot? I ask
It worries me dawn to dusk
It wakes me when I'm sleeping
This person would have to have luck.

I've dodged some bullets before
They were whizzing past my head
When I hit the ground I rolled and turned
And managed to shoot them dead.

So if I end up in that coffin one day
No one around to cry
Only the priest to say his word
And nobody to say goodbye

So if a bullet hits me one day
It might be a little too soon
I'll fall to the ground, fly up to Heaven
And it would be like nobody knew.

Lenny Whelan (11)
Mayfield Secondary School, Portsmouth

The Chernobyl Children

Waiting for the minibus
Excited, nervous,
Practising last minute Russian.
For the girls will be here any moment.
The girls who are part of our family for the month.
Girls who are on a respite holiday
From the radiation at home.

The bus is here!
They all start getting off,
Looking scared
I watch them smiling,
Wondering which two are ours.

We're introduced by the leader.
I hug the girls and smile.
They look scared and nervous
As I introduce myself in Russian.
They smile at the thought
I can speak bits of their language.

We all climb in the car
And begin to drive home.
I look forward to the month ahead
Knowing we'll have laughs,
But at the same time
Dread the day they leave,
Knowing many tears will be shed
As they climb on the minibus
For the last time.

Rosie Lunn (13)
Mayfield Secondary School, Portsmouth

My Cat Timmy

My cat Timmy is not a clever cat,
We call him Dimmy,
Going in the washing machine,
Playing around,
My cat Timmy.

My cat Timmy is so fluffy,
His soft fur against my cheek,
Whenever I'm ill,
Oh my cat Timmy.

My cat Timmy,
Has a hunger for trouble,
Knocking down the vases whenever he can,
Oh my cat Timmy.

When he's cold and outside,
He wants to be tucked up in bed with Mummy,
My cat is crazy, annoying and mad,
But I love him anyway,
His white fluffy beard
And his Harry Potter scar-shaped marking,
His warming touch and his love of TV,
Oh my cat Timmy is so dimmy.

Lauren Sharpe (12)
Mayfield Secondary School, Portsmouth

Circus

Well, there's horses, of courses.
And clowns and horses, of courses.
And clowns that flounder around, of courses.
And clowns who flounder and fall around, of courses.
With small tiny cars, home to the clowns
who fall and crash and flounder around, of courses.
And tiny elephants and giant cars where the clowns
who fall, crash and flounder around can leap and bound, of courses.
And tiny elephants and massive cars and short men on stilts
and with tall men on bikes and women on tightropes
with lights on who watch the clowns as they leap and bound
and flounder around, of courses.
And horses, of courses.

Oliver Hurst (15)
Mayfield Secondary School, Portsmouth

The Toy Shop

Whizzing round the toy shop
I find some wonderful things.

The army toys are fighting
The little boys are climbing
The toy cars are racing
The tiny girls are painting
The Toy Story characters are escaping
And the little farm is working.

That's the wonderful things
Happening in the toy shop.

Brooke Critchett (11)
Mayfield Secondary School, Portsmouth

Diva Fever

D ancing all day
I n bright clothing
V ery energetic
A lways smiling

F orever entertaining
E xcellent performers
V ery cool
E xcellent audition
R eally gutted they went out.

Shawnie Guy (13)
Mayfield Secondary School, Portsmouth

What Matters To You?

Sunken eyes, a skeletal figure
Black lungs or a busted liver.

How can you live with a friend in need
Dying of an illness or addicted to weed?

How can you just sit there at home
When your friend could be hurting, lost or alone?

If they need help there's hope in your heart
But when you're rejected how can you start?

'Don't worry, I'm fine,' that's what you said
But you look as if you're on your deathbed.

How can you help when you're pushed away?
But your friend is being led astray.

What matters to me
Is my friends' health and safety.

We'll make it through thick and thin, no fear
Don't worry I'll always be here.

Rachel Dixon (13)
Mount Grace School, Potters Bar

What Matters To Me

H ear the taunts from the boys in the playground
O pting to ignore rather than understand.
M any are in this horrible condition.
O bviously it must be a problem.
P ressing on and on about his opinions,
H arassing him day and night.
O n the outside a normal person,
B ut on the inside, falling, dying, deteriorating.
I nside is a bomb.
A ticking time bomb waiting to implode.

I mplode right over his heart,
S o he could never love another.

C ontinuing the bullying,
R ealise that it hurts.
U nderstand it's cruel.
E very day he's scared to leave the house.
L aughter fills his empty brain.

A nother doesn't cease tormenting him,
N ever thinking of consequences.
D on't laugh.

D on't stare.
E verybody deserves an opinion.
M ine could be different to yours,
E verybody's different
A nd it shouldn't even matter.
N ever ever should someone take their own life,
I t's not worth it.
N ever harass because you don't understand.
G o take your homophobia somewhere else.

Trey Thomas (13)
Mount Grace School, Potters Bar

The Death Of Unrequited Lovers

The grey clouds gathered to play their god.
A tear slid down her cheek as the games had begun.
She whimpered slowly but fell into silence,
She had just lived a life full of defiance.
And all that was left was a graveyard of memories.
Such a bunch of well written felonies
But in that box remained one memory.
A familiar face but a horrible chemistry.

Oh what a terrible unforgiveable mistake.
Her love for him was so unbelievably fake.
She was struck by Satan, into the pity of sorrow.
Not even God could save her tomorrow.
Already the damage had been done
But to her it was just a bit of fun.
But in that box remained one memory.
A familiar face but a horrible chemistry.

The blood on his body was already stained
And the love in his heart was already pained.
The shatter of glass did the job.
He never saw the bottle being lobbed.
She stood there and laughed and waved goodbye,
The love she had for him was just a very big lie.
But in that box remained one memory.
A familiar face but a horrible chemistry.

It started to sink in and she had brutally killed him
And now the rest of her life looked let's say pretty dim.
The bruises on her arms did not persuade the crowds
And the corpse on the floor had been covered with a shroud.
She was thrown in a cage like the animal she was
But she could not be tamed, because of the fighting mobs.
But in that box remained one memory,
A familiar face but a horrible chemistry.

The lawyer protested but the deal was done and dusted.
So she agreed guilty for being terribly lustred.
Her face seemed to age
But her mind still engaged.
The demon within her came out to see the world,

She will never be the same, that poor frightened little girl
But in that box remained one memory.
A familiar face but a horrible chemistry.

Her health deteriorated and she was mostly bedridden,
And like a secret from the world she was very well hidden.
Healthy or really sick, no one seemed to care,
She was a monster so not even an interest was dared.
She died alone and in a lot of pain,
Some people could have said she was mentally insane,
But in that box remained one memory,
Hidden from the world, that deathly chemistry.

Sarah Evans (13)
Mount Grace School, Potters Bar

What Matters To Me

I don't know what to write you see,
Because there's a lot that matters to me,

What matters to me is the power of love,
It is the sun glittering, shining above,
Love is an hourglass disintegrating in time,
If I reject your love you'll no longer be mine,

What matters to me is my family of four,
My mum, dad, sister, I don't need anymore,

What matters to me are the people around,
Laughing, joking, I love that sound,
Everyone is different, we are all equal,
We may not look the same but everyone is people,

I need to stop now, time has run out,
Not really, I'm kidding, my pen's run out!
But let me say this before I go,
There is a little more I need you to know,

There is so much more that matters to me,
So this is not the end of my story . . .

Katie Scales (13)
Mount Grace School, Potters Bar

She Is Love

She is simple
She is shy
She is waiting for the right guy
For what she wishes to find
And what she is not getting.

Do not be discreet for the first moment you meet
She will not say one word
But will look at you with no emotion
What you are thinking is all lies

She is not really shy
Inside she is bold and full with spark
One day she may let you into her heart.

She is confusing
She makes no sense
She's a human
She is the best
Take your time to understand her
And she shall let you into her life
Soon she will be your best friend.

She is your soulmate
She is your life
One day you shall ask her
'Will you be my lawful wedded wife?'

Now you are married
Now you are old
This is how your story is told
But remember this
The first time you meet
The first time you speak
The first time you dance as she fell to your feet.

When you fell into love
There was no way out
She's now happy
She will always be
Thanks to you and her family
She is your love.

Sammi Patterson (13)
Mount Grace School, Potters Bar

What Matters To Me?

To me a life without music
Is like a painting without colour.

To me a life without friends
Is like a daughter without a mother.

A book without words,
Who would read that?

A photo album without pictures,
An empty flat.

To me loneliness is like a beat with no rhythm,
A universe with no solar system.

An August day without a sun,
A monastery without a nun.

A church song book without a hymn,
A glass of tonic without gin.

To me going to sleep is like a nightmare,
To me life without you is just a scare.

To me life with no family is silence,
Dull and quiet,
Just silence . . .

Macey Reynolds (14)
Mount Grace School, Potters Bar

What Matters To Me?

Somewhere, someone is crying
Someone they love is slowly dying
A gunshot to the chest
I will leave it there at best
Many people have this in heart
Many people are torn apart
Kissing your loved ones, off he goes
All the sadness in their eyes shows
Will he return? Will he come home?
I sit here and think alone
Why does this happen to people today?
Why doesn't war go away?
It haunts us like an old ghost
Both are what some people fear the most
Tears fall from unseen eyes
And in their ears they hear the cries
Of their friends who they lost
All comes at a hurtful cost
These men have so much fear, I know
But enough courage not to let it show
And one by one they all fall
They die for us, for us all
Why don't people stop and think?
Many people are on the brink
Of death or a lot of pain
Many have gone lame
This is what matters to me, my friend
Why can't war just end?

Emily Toye (13)
Mount Grace School, Potters Bar

What Matters To Me?

What matters to me? Lots I have to say.
Football, cricket, rugby, tennis and other sports I play.
All the gadgets in my room, laptop, phone, TV,
Even my comfortable, cosy bed. They all matter to me.

What matters to me? Walking my dog in the park,
Chasing after Bailey and listening to him bark.
Beating my dad and brother on the PS3,
Looking at their faces when it's 3-0 to me.

What matters to me? Being a goalkeeper.
Making flying, fantastic saves but other things deeper,
Like being with and talking to friends and family
Helping them and listening to them because they all matter to me.

What matters to me? Breakfast, lunch and dinner.
My dad cooking meals like a Michelin award winner.
Going on holiday to swim in the pools and the sea.
Relaxing on the beach, they all matter to me.

What matters to me? The presents I get.
On my birthday and Christmas, also my pet.
Enjoying myself, having a laugh and being happy.
Every one of these things matter to me.

Hadley Caswell (13)
Mount Grace School, Potters Bar

What Matters To You

The things that matter are my friends and family.
My friends are sweet, never let me down.
Great fun and always messing around.
My family is strange, divorced and married again.
But life goes on, never the same,
New buildings, new places, relax, just slow down.
But that's my life running around!

Nicholas Stringer (13)
Mount Grace School, Potters Bar

What Matters To You

Are you afraid of illness? Disease? Cancer or diabetes?
The fear of your father dying and your mother crying?
Are you scared?
Are you upset that you haven't got a PlayStation 3
Or that you're not at home playing Wii?
You cry over no sweets
Even though there's people dying of heat, dehydration.
That b***h who killed your mum is waiting at the station
For the next innocent person to step round the corner.
Are you scared?
For any mourner that is upset just think you are not alone,
There are many kids out there danger prone,
They die over guns and crimes
Never get the chance to shimmer and shine.

People die and people cry,
Are you scared? Because I am.
Get away from it while you can!

Maria Harris (13)
Mount Grace School, Potters Bar

What Matters To Me?

She is my best friend!
This is because she is fun and so cool!
She loves me and I love her so much more!
She is funny and I have the best memories with her!
We are both 'brace faces' which makes us an awesome pair!
We share loads of secrets and I trust her not to tell.
There is so much more to tell but there's not enough time,
So I only have one question,
Do you know who this girl is?
It's my best friend, Hannah Crick!

Emily Allen (13)
Mount Grace School, Potters Bar

What Matters Most To Me Is Love

The flapping wings of a white crystal dove
Represents my favourite thing - love.
Love is power, love is a thing,
Love makes you feel as if you are a king.

Love is a beating heart,
Love is what also breaks your heart!
Love can make you fall apart
But the thing that matters most to me is your sweet heart.

With Cupid flying above
You are my true love,
Cupid's arrow may hit you in the arse
But I can make you fall in love, fast.

Love is you,
Love is me
And this is my story.

Maisie Clancy (13)
Mount Grace School, Potters Bar

The Thing That Matters Most To Me

The thing that matters most to me
Are dolphins leaping through the sea,
Their flukes flapping widely,
Their hearts are very close to me,
That's what matters to me.

The thing that matters most to me
Is my best friend Emily D,
I've known her since Year 1 you see,
Just like Chiara and Rachel D,
They're what matter most to me.

I have written my poem that I had to do,
So now tell me, what matters most to you?

Amy Lawrence (13)
Mount Grace School, Potters Bar

What Matters To Me

What matters to me is love
What matters to me is hate
What matters to me is destiny
What matters to me is fate.
What matters to me is not what I have learnt, but what I have taught.
What matters to me is not my competence, but my character.
What matters to me is not how many people I know,
But how many people will feel a lasting loss when I have gone.
What matters to me are not my memories,
But the memories that live in those who loved me.
What matters to me are the little things
That make life complete
Like simply knowing that you're here
Now it's very clear
What really matters to me,
Is my love for you is true.

Amber Laing (13)
Mount Grace School, Potters Bar

Perfection

A flowing mane,
A perfect stride,
Hard to tame,
To be ridden with pride,

Two delicate ears,
Four shapely hooves,
Lives for years,
Just look at it move,

What am I?
I hear you ask,
Well I am,
A beautiful horse . . .

Chiara Merlo (13)
Mount Grace School, Potters Bar

Life

What matters to me is life itself,
The eating, the drinking, the love and health,
The kindness, the joy, the family and friends,
If it was up to me the positives never end.

There are some things that are negative in my life,
The wars, the affairs, the crime of gun and knife,
Violence is another negative thing,
Stabbing, the rape, racism and killing.

So overall life is OK,
But I think I waste it, day after day.
We don't actually realise how precious life is,
Life is wasted, wasted life is.

Emily Pack [13]
Mount Grace School, Potters Bar

What Matters To You?

I love her because she is smelly and is a brace face like me,
I can tell her anything and she won't laugh at me,
She twists and flicks, a hard nut all over,
And this is why she is my smelliest forever.

Been together what feels like forever,
Never seeing what we are together,
Best friends now and forever,
Nothing can break us, we are the best pair ever.

Hannah Crick [13]
Mount Grace School, Potters Bar

Making It Up

She looks in the mirror.
Her clinical eye
Spots the flaws.

First, concealer.
Together with foundation
It hides red blemishes.

Then the eyeliner.
Thick black rings
Give her racoons' eyes.

Mascara too,
Lashings of it,
To create an alluring glance.

Add come eyeshadow.
Delicate peacock shades,
That shimmer in the light.

Don't forget blusher!
Blending in rose,
The illusion of cheekbones.

Finally, lipstick.
Her pouting duck's beak
Turns as red as a London bus.

She looks in the mirror,
Likes what she sees.
Blows a kiss.

Perfect.
Flawless.
Fake.

Tamara Stojanovic (16)
Oxford High School, Oxford

The Dancers

They dance at the chiming,
As the hands turn swiftly,
A tempo unrecorded
By anybody's clock.

They dance at the chiming,
As the hands turn swiftly,
The thirteenth hour announced
In nobody's clock.

They dance at the chiming,
As the hands turn swiftly,
And no one is watching
The dancers are unwatched.

They dance at the chiming,
As the hands turn swiftly,
A tempo unrecorded
By anybody's clock.

Laura Rosenheim (12)
Oxford High School, Oxford

Home

This is not my home -
These curtains do not bear my lop-sided seams,
The smell is too clinical, too white.
I walk around the garden,
Lazily kept.
In a state of suspended animation, I look into the cracks in the wall
To find something which I could claim for my own.
Forget-me-nots.
Later I return to this bedroom
With a bed that does not moan as I turn over.
I look out of the window, in my orange streetlight glory,
Shrouded in cigarette smoke.
I trawl through the night to find something,
Anything that takes me home.

Poppy Simmonds (17)
Oxford High School, Oxford

After A Rainfall

Today it rained.
Now mist wanders
My garden, slow,
As if confused
As to how it
Came to be there.
The little snails
Ventured out,
Creeping,
Afraid to leave
Their homes behind,
So they took them
Along for the journey.
I saw a frog,
Sitting, thinking,
Pondering the world
And its folly.
He blinked,
Once,
Twice,
Then jumped and was gone.

Things change after
A rainfall.
Everything is fresh,
Newly minted,
Bold in its chance
To begin again,
All the old mistakes
Washed away.

I wish to stand
Outside, with all
The plants and their
Wild inhabitants,
And let the rain
Leap from the sky
To my skin,
And shimmer along
My limbs and wash

My mistakes away,
Cleanse and absolve
Me of my sins,
Like holy water.

Abigail Gibbs (17)
Peter Symonds College, Winchester

She Is Gone

The box has
sat there,
ever since she . . . left.
It was her box.
A box meant to hold
playing cards.

She liked cards.
She liked going to
the bridge club every
so often
to play with her friends.

The box doesn't hold cards
now.
It holds her jewellery.
Necklaces, bracelets, rings.

When
I miss her,
I open it.
The smell of her
still lingers there,
and she is here.

But when
I close it
again,
she is not here,
she is gone.

Julia Parison (14)
Prior's Field School, Godalming

My Trip To The Death Factory

We file in silence.
Stones make us stumble,
Where others have fallen.
Dust clings to our clothes
Seeking salvation and remembrance.
Sombre mouths are set,
Eyes absorbing every
Bullet holed brick.
Like dumb children we follow
No sound made
No protest wailed
No chance of escape.

Before us the wasteland
Of grass gorges itself
On the charred remains of soil,
Birdsong is absent from this register.
Rows of wooden huts hunch in salute.
The raw moans of the dying are mimicked
By the wind,
Waiting with our nostrils flexed
For the foul smell to seep up
And roast a mental picture.

Nothing comes,
No rescue, just endless days of the torture and labour,
Now those who march the path of the dead
Are tourists armed with camera and tissue packet.
No gun,
No fist impacts on the frail bodies anymore.

Missing is the scent of death.
The shrieks of those torn from the breast of family
And dragged to chamber or doctor,
Remain clinging to the wind which surges between the bones of memory.
It screams in our faces of the horror it has been forced to watch,
It will never rest, stripped of life, dignity.

To think we have wandered
Where they were butchered
We left through gates where they were hoarded between,

And we escaped the concrete bunkers
Which enveloped their lives in gas-filled death.
These souls now wander the endless realms of our minds,
Trying to find justification between our folds of humanity.

Caitlin McConnell (16)
Prior's Field School, Godalming

Maddie

I'm sad and confused
And don't know what to do

I run down the black, plain road
And feel you tugging at the lead
As you urge to go faster
I look down. Nothing there.

I walk up the dusty path
And hear you digging a deep hole
Wishing hard to catch rabbits
I look right. Nothing there.

I jump over the clear stream
Hear a splash and feel a wet spray
As you play in the water
I look behind. Nothing there.

I trudge through the green meadow
Hear barking and the swish of grass
As you chase your own tail
I look left. Nothing there.

I walk down the muddy slope
And smell lumps of dug up earth
As you coat yourself in mud
I look up. Nothing there.

I get back. Friends comfort me.
But they don't know what it's like
To lose a best friend.

Genevieve Lebus (12)
Prior's Field School, Godalming

Autistic

Baked beans
Canned tomatoes
Tins of soup knocked
Down
Thud! Smash! Roll away
No point in saying no Mom.
Don't stomp your foot just say OK
Spinning faster now
The noise rings through his brain
Don't cry
Be safe.

Four years later
Now he's ten, or is he?
Yes, you're right
He's not the same and knows it
Now
Point yes or no
Don't say it aloud
The words just won't come out
Special, different, someone else
No one seems to like it
That's not fair though
He can't fight it.

Sixteen candles blown away
With help
Of course
Ask him how he feels
Can't tell you
Beautiful mind, words to say
Can't tell you
He's just shy?
Don't be ashamed
It'll all be better
Soon.

I'll grow up
I'll find a cure
I know how to help.

You matter to me.

Emily Milton (14)
Prior's Field School, Godalming

Once Alive, Now Deceased

I had never experienced the death of a loved one,
Only empathised with others,
Until now

The feeling of grief and frustration
Manifests inside me,
It has devoured any morale,
Consumed any self control,
Absorbed any kindness
And sucked out any love.
It feeds off any happiness
That I endure.
It has constricted itself around my body,
Entwined in the brain,
Slowly it is eating me alive.
It has engulfed me bit by bit
And now I am just a shell.
It has attacked my mind,
And condensed it down,
It makes many a man go mad,
But I have fought the temptation to give up.

The only antidote,
For the suffering, is love.
Love is the most powerful weapon.
It is radiated from those around you,
And gradually it will defeat the anger and sadness.

Elena Georgiakakis (12)
Prior's Field School, Godalming

Silence

'What matters to me,'
said the teacher to us,
'is having a quiet class,
just for once!'
We carried on,
a mere glance then
back to our noisy chatter.
Talking about the weekend,
what we want to happen on X Factor.
Texting under the tables,
paper aeroplanes flying across the room.
A few squeals as someone
sticks their hand in some gum.
'Please!' Her voice grows louder,
'Silence!'

But who does she think we are?
We are no politicians,
who sit all day,
listening to speeches,
drinking coffee, silent.
Or no soldiers,
still, standing regimented,
silent.
We are a pack of animals,
trying to break free from our cage,
unable to be quiet just for once.
We are a flock of birds
longing to fly free,
getting louder and louder.
'Detention!'
   . . . Silence!

Jasmine Smith [14]
Prior's Field School, Godalming

Featured Poets:
DEAD POETS
AKA Mark Grist & MC Mixy

Mark Grist and MC Mixy joined forces to become the 'Dead Poets' in 2008.

Since then Mark and Mixy have been challenging the preconceptions of poetry and hip hop across the country. As 'Dead Poets', they have performed in venues ranging from nightclubs to secondary schools; from festivals to formal dinners. They've appeared on Radio 6 Live with Steve Merchant, they've been on a national tour with Phrased and Confused and debuted their show at the 2010 Edinburgh Fringe, which was a huge success.

Both Mark and Mixy work on solo projects as well as working together as the 'Dead Poets'. Both have been Peterborough's Poet Laureate, with Mixy holding the title for 2010.

The 'Dead Poets' are available for workshops in your school as well as other events. Visit www.deadpoetry.co.uk for further information and to contact the guys!

Read on to pick up some fab writing tips!

Your WORKSHOPS

In these workshops we are going to look at writing styles and examine some literary techniques that the 'Dead Poets' use. Grab a pen, and let's go!

Rhythm Workshop

Rhythm in writing is like the beat in music. Rhythm is when certain words are produced more forcefully than others, and may be held for longer duration. The repetition of a pattern is what produces a 'rhythmic effect'. The word rhythm comes from the Greek meaning of 'measured motion'.

Count the number of syllables in your name. Then count the number of syllables in the following line, which you write in your notepad: 'My horse, my horse, will not eat grass'.

Now, highlight the longer sounding syllables and then the shorter sounding syllables in a different colour.

Di dum, di dum, di dum, di dum is a good way of summing this up.

You should then try to write your own lines that match this rhythm. You have one minute to see how many you can write!

Examples include:
'My cheese smells bad because it's hot'
and
'I do not like to write in rhyme'.

For your poem, why don't you try to play with the rhythm? Use only longer beats or shorter beats? Create your own beat and write your lines to this?

Rhyme Workshop

Start off with the phrase 'I'd rather be silver than gold' in your notepad. and see if you can come up with lines that rhyme with it -
'I'd rather have hair than be bald'
'I'd rather be young than be old'
'I'd rather be hot than cold'
'I'd rather be bought than sold'

Also, pick one of these words and see how many rhymes you can find:

Rose

Wall

Warm

Danger

What kinds of rhymes did you come up with? Are there differences in rhymes? Do some words rhyme more cleanly than others? Which do you prefer and why?

Lists Workshop

Game - you (and you can ask your friends or family too) to write as many reasons as possible for the following topics:

Annoying things about siblings

The worst pets ever

The most disgusting ingredients for a soup you can think of

Why not try writing a poem with the same first 2, 3 or 4 words?

I am ...

Or

I love it when ...

Eg:

I am a brother

I am a listener

I am a collector of secrets

I am a messer of bedrooms.

Onomatopoeia Workshop

Divide a sheet of A4 paper into 8 squares.

You then have thirty seconds to draw/write what could make the following sounds:

Splash	Ping
Drip	Bang
Rip	Croak
Crack	Splash

Now try writing your own ideas of onomatopoeia. Why might a writer include onomatopoeia in their writing?

Repetition Workshop

Come up with a list of words/ phrases, aim for at least 5. You now must include one of these words in your piece at least 6 times. You aren't allowed to place these words/ phrases at the beginning of any of the lines.

Suggested words/phrases:

Why

Freedom

Laughing

That was the best day ever

I can't find the door

I'm in trouble again

The best

Workshop
POETRY 101

Below is a poem written especially for Poetry Matters, by MC Mixy.
Why not try and write some more poems of your own?

What is Matter?

© MC Mixy

What matters to me may not be the same things that matter to you
You may not agree with my opinion mentality or attitude
The order in which I line up my priorities to move
Choose to include my view and do what I do due to my mood
And state of mind
I make the time to place the lines on stacks of paper and binds
Concentrate on my artwork hard I can't just pass and scrape behind
Always keep close mates of mine that make things right
And even those who can't … just cos I love the way they can try
What matters to me is doing things the right way
It's tough this game of life we play what we think might stray from what
others might say
In this world of individuality we all wanna bring originality
Live life and drift through casually but the vicious reality is
Creativity is unique
Opinions will always differ but if you figure you know the truth, speak
So many things matter to me depending on how tragically deep you wanna
go
I know I need to defy gravity on this balance beam
As I laugh and breathe draft and read map the scene practise piece smash
the beat and graphic release
Visual and vocal it's a standard procedure
Have to believe and don't bite the hand when it feeds ya

If you wanna be a leader you need to stay out of the pen where the sheep
are
The things that matter to me are
My art and my friends
That will stay from the start to the end
People will do things you find hard to amend
Expect the attacks and prepare you gotta be smart to defend
I put my whole heart in the blend the mass is halved yet again
I'm marked by my pen a big fish fighting sharks of men
In a small pond
Dodging harpoons and nets hooks and predators tryna dismember ya
I won't let them I won't get disheartened I can fend for myself
As long as I'm doing what's important
I'm my mind where I'm supported is a just cause to be supporting
In these appalling hard times I often find myself falling when
Only two aspects of my life keep me sane and allow me to stand tall again
Out of all of them two is a small number
It's a reminder I remind ya to hold necessity and let luxury fall under
Try to avoid letting depression seep through
Take the lesson we actually need a lot less than we think we do
So what matters to you?
They may be similar to things that matter to me
I'm actually lacking the need of things I feel would help me to succeed
Though I like to keep it simple, I wanna love, I wanna breed
I'm one of many individuals in this world where importance fluctuates and
varies
Things that matter will come and go
But the ones that stay for long enough must be worth keeping close
If you're not sure now don't watch it you'll know when you need to know
Me, I think I know now … yet I feel and fear I don't.

Turn overleaf for a poem by Mark Grist
and some fantastic hints and tips!

Workshop
POETRY 101

What Tie Should I Wear Today?

© Mark Grist

I wish I had a tie that was suave and silk and slick,
One with flair, that's debonair and would enchant with just one flick,
Yeah, I'd like that … a tie that's hypnotizing,
I'd be very restrained and avoid womanising,
But all the lady teachers would still say 'Mr Grist your tie's so charming!'
As I cruise into their classrooms with it striking and disarming.
At parents' evenings my tie's charm would suffice,
In getting mums to whisper as they leave 'Your English teacher seems nice!'

Or maybe an evil-looking tie - one that's the business,
Where students will go 'Watch out! Mr Grist is
on the prowl with that evil tie.'
The one that cornered Josh and then ripped out his eye.
Yeah no one ever whispers, no one ever sniggers,
Or my tie would rear up and you'd wet your knickers.
Maybe one girl just hasn't heard the warning,
Cos she overslept and turned up late to school that morning,
And so I'd catch her in my lesson yawning … oh dear.
I'd try to calm it down, but this tie's got bad ideas.
It'd size the girl up and then just as she fears,
Dive in like a serpent snapping at her ears.
There'd be a scream, some blood and lots and lots of tears,
And she wouldn't be able to yawn again for years.

Or maybe … a tie that everyone agrees is mighty fine
And people travel from miles around to gawp at the design
I'd like that … a tie that pushes the boundaries of tieware right up to the limit
It'd make emos wipe their tears away while chavs say 'It's wicked innit?'
and footy lads would stop me with 'I'd wear that if I ever won the cup.'
And I'd walk through Peterborough to slapped backs, high fives, thumbs up
While monosyllabic teenagers would just stand there going 'Yup.'

I don't know. I'd never be sure which of the three to try
As any decision between them would always end a tie.

Tips and Advice for PERFORMING Your Poem

So you've written your poem, now how about performing it.
Whether you read your poem for the first time in front of your class, school or strangers at an open mic event or poetry slam, these tips will help you make the best of your performance.

Breathe and try to relax.

Every poet that reads in front of people for the first time feels a bit nervous, when you're there you are in charge and nothing serious can go wrong.

People at poetry slams or readings are there to support the poets. They really are!

If you can learn your poem off by heart that is brilliant, however having a piece of paper or notebook with your work in is fine, though try not to hide behind these.

It's better to get some eye contact with the audience.
If you're nervous find a friendly face to focus on.

Try to read slowly and clearly and enjoy your time in the spotlight.

Don't rush up to the microphone, make sure it's at the right height for you and if you need it adjusted ask one of the team around you.

Before you start, stand up as straight as you can and get your body as comfortable as you can and remember to hold your head up.

The microphone can only amplify what what's spoken into it; if you're very loud you might end up deafening people and if you only whisper or stand too far away you won't be heard.

When you say something before your poem, whether that's hello or just the title of your poem, try and have a listen to how loud you sound. If you're too quiet move closer to the microphone, if you're too loud move back a bit.

Remember to breathe! Don't try to say your poem so quickly you can't find time to catch your breath.

And finally, **enjoy!**

Poetry FACTS

Here are a selection of fascinating poetry facts!

No word in the English language rhymes with 'MONTH'.

William Shakespeare was born on 23rd April 1564 and died on 23rd April 1616.

The haiku is one of the shortest forms of poetic writing.
Originating in Japan, a haiku poem is only seventeen syllables, typically broken down into three lines of five, seven and five syllables respectively.

The motto of the Globe Theatre was 'totus mundus agit histrionem' (the whole world is a playhouse).

The Children's Laureate award was an idea by Ted Hughes and Michael Morpurgo.

The 25th January each year is Burns' Night, an occasion in honour of Scotland's national poet Robert Burns.

Spike Milligan's 'On the Ning Nang Nong' was voted the UK's favourite comic poem in 1998.

Did you know *onomatopoeia* means the word you use sounds like the word you are describing – like the rain *pitter-patters* or the snow *crunches* under my foot.

'Go' is the shortest complete sentence in the English language.

Did you know rhymes were used in olden days to help people remember the news? Ring-o'-roses is about the Plague!

The Nursery Rhyme 'Old King Cole' is based on a real king and a real historical event. King Cole is supposed to have been an actual monarch of Britain who ruled around 200 A.D.

Edward Lear popularised the limerick with his poem 'The Owl and the Pussy-Cat'.

Lewis Carroll's poem 'The Jabberwocky' is written in nonsense style.

POEM – noun

1. a composition in verse, esp. one that is characterized by a highly developed artistic form and by the use of heightened language and rhythm to express an intensely imaginative interpretation of the subject.

122

Poetry TIPS

We have compiled some helpful tips for you budding poets...

In order to write poetry, read lots of poetry!

Keep a notebook with you at all times so you can write whenever (and wherever) inspiration strikes.

Every line of a poem should be important to the poem and interesting to read. A poem with only 3 great lines should be 3 lines long.

Use an online rhyming dictionary to improve your vocabulary.

Use free workshops and help sheets to learn new poetry styles.

Experiment with visual patterns - does your written poetry create a good pattern on the page?

Try to create pictures in the reader's mind - aim to fire the imagination.

Develop your voice. Become comfortable with how you write.

Listen to criticism, and try to learn from it, but don't live or die by it.

Say what you want to say, let the reader decide what it means.

Notice what makes other's poetry memorable. Capture it, mix it up and make it your own. (Don't copy other's work word for word!)

Go wild. Be funny. Be serious. Be whatever you want!

Grab hold of something you feel - anything you feel - and write it.

The more you write, the more you develop. Write poetry often.

Use your imagination, your own way of seeing.

Feel free to write a bad poem, it will develop your 'voice'.

Did you know ...?

'The Epic of Gilgamesh' was written thousands of years ago in Mesopotamia and is the oldest poem on record.

Wordsmith

The *premier* magazine
for creative young people

A platform for your imagination and creativity. Showcase your ideas and have your say. Welcome to a place where like-minded young people express their personalities and individuality knows no limits.

For further information visit ***www.youngwriters.co.uk***.

A peek into Wordsmith world ...

Poetry and Short Stories

We feature both themed and non-themed work every issue. Previous themes have included; dreams and aspirations, superhero stories and ghostly tales.

Next Generation Author

This section devotes two whole pages to one of our readers' work. The perfect place to showcase a selection of your poems, stories or both!

Guest Author Features & Workshops

Interesting and informative tutorials on different styles of poetry and creative writing. Famous authors and illustrators share their advice with us on how to create gripping stories and magical picturebooks. Novelists like Michael Morpurgo and Celia Rees go under the spotlight to answer our questions.

The fun doesn't stop there ...

Every issue we tell you what events are coming up across the country. We keep you up to date with the latest film and book releases and we feature some yummy recipes to help feed the brain and get the creative juices flowing.

So with all this and more, Wordsmith is *the* magazine to be reading.

If you are too young for Wordsmith magazine or have a younger friend who enjoys creative writing, then check out Scribbler!. Scribbler! is for 7-11 year-olds and is jam-packed full of brilliant features, young writers' work, competitions and interviews too. For further information check out ***www.youngwriters.co.uk*** or ask an adult to call us on (01733) 890066.

To get an adult to subscribe to either magazine for you,
ask them to visit the website or give us a call.

What Matters To Me?

The wimpy whisper of the wind
As it cascades through the air.
Wrapped up, he stands there, near the bin,
And waits for your care.

He wants to play but you're not there.
He moans and yells and shouts.
Eventually you decide to be fair
And join him, ready to go out.

You walk through a lonesome road
On your way to the woods.
Holding his ball, old football shoes
And his bag of goods.

Yippee you've finally arrived,
And he's acting like a young boy
The journey you have tactfully survived
After all his singing and joy.

A ball flies into the distant space
And lands lonely at your feet.
You kick it back, with a smile on your face.
Here comes the heat.

The leaves crunch as they are stamped on
By his big and battering boots.
The moaning and irritation of your son
As he gets tangled in the roots.

Drip, drop as tears tumble off his face,
Trickling into the imaginary sea.
They gain speed like it's a race.
Everything's music to me.

Rebeccah Webber (14)
Prior's Field School, Godalming

What Matters To Me?

What matters to me?
Well, music is a part of my life,
Can make me feel great, or bring out my strife,
It can elate your mind,
And all of mankind will understand.

What matters to me? Sweets.
When you suck and chew and sigh,
And they melt into a divine . . . oh my,
My mouth is watering now,
It would even for a cow,
But everyone will understand.

What matters to me, hmm . . .
Nature surrounds us,
It is the essence of the Earth,
Though I must say,
Earth has an awfully large girth.
But what we do to it,
Well what's the worth?
I'm sure you'll understand.

What about you?
Now you know me.
Tell me what matters to you,
So that I can see!

Holly James [13]
Prior's Field School, Godalming

Colour Left Me Blind

I once used to know,
green grass that protruded out of the dark, brown, sloppy mud.
Pale, green, endless skies painted with soft, white cloud cushions.
Scarlet that oozed from her lips, soft to touch.
Silver iridescent moonlight that we used to bathe in.
Piercing orange that soaked, soothed and brightened the land.
Glossy pink of each velvet petal on Valentine's Day.
My pure reflection in the mirror,
the photo of our honeymoon, my destiny.

October 20th Gone. Vanished.
Disappeared. Evaporated. Drained.
Colour left me,
blind.

Now all I can sense,
are silhouettes flickering here and there.
Shadows stomping around,
shapes are fuzzy. Unclear,
like a TV with no signal.
Sound but no sight.
Unsure where to place your next step.
Never knowing,
when a rainbow shines before you.

Kate Alexander (14)
Prior's Field School, Godalming

You Matter To Me

You are there for me, whatever I do
I know I will always be in your heart, like a permanent tattoo.
When I see you, I get a warm feeling in my heart
That will never feel the same, like an unique work of art.
When I am upset, and I cry at night,
As soon as I see you, you always make me feel alright.

Chesca Loggia (13)
Prior's Field School, Godalming

Goodnight Grandma

The pain, it ran down my body,
Through my chest.
Like paint splattered on a wall.
It ran and ran.
My heart skipped a beat,
It stopped stone cold.

My heart was torn,
I felt a thud,
I caught my breath.
There was a sudden light.

Her face was pale,
Her lips were blue,
Her heart stopped beating
Mine had too.

I cried and cried
But no one could hear,
The tears on my face
Weren't that clear.

At last I saw a beautiful sight
I took her hand
And kissed her goodnight.

Lucy Edwards (12)
Prior's Field School, Godalming

Out Of Reality

Begin.

Big bold chords
hammer over the oak scented
ivory keys. My nimble fingers glide
effortlessly across, leaving a delicate path
of high-pitched melodic notes. The next chapter.
Ping! The highest C is pressed, filling the milling room
with a sweet taste. Compressed and rising, the keys live
in a world of their own. Down, up, left, right. The next one plays,
bouncing on around my mind. They stand to attention,
awaiting my hunger to touch them. I just listen;
the luscious sounds transfer you to another world,
travelling to another place where everything is
perfect. The picturesque landscape full of
too-bright-to-be-real flowers in a
country field. And I feel like dancing,
dancing to the music.

A round of applause.

Kimi Worsdell (14)
Prior's Field School, Godalming

Life Is What Matters

Life brings the future and holds the past,
It also holds our memories, both good and bad.
Without life there would be nothing,
Nothing at all.
Dreams would disappear, nightmares and all.
Life is why we are here,
Even if it can bring us tears.
It can break our hearts,
But it can give us the smile that washes our sadness away.

Rebecca Gwyther (13)
Prior's Field School, Godalming

Tildy

She was so beautiful,
So sweet and kind,
Amazing in every single way,
But my poor best friend,
She was given a horrible illness.

She battled with this illness for months,
Then suddenly she was better,
The doctors had got rid of all the cancer cells,
Well that's what they thought.

My friend was back to her normal life,
Happy and sweet as ever.

Then my dear friend got ill again,
The doctors didn't get rid of all the cancer cells,
She got very, very ill
And had this battle all over again.

My best friend is now playing with the fairies up in Heaven
And will be with me, in my heart, forever.

Alicia Newland (12)
Prior's Field School, Godalming

Sweet War

Through bitter murmurs, words begrudge
as I bequeath discontentment, as we trudge.
Hands clasped around the bayonet,
our gnarled brown boots in mud swamps set.

Flares alight! Amnesia consumes
as comrades fall lifeless in corruption of fumes.
Blood gargles and gutters, to the direst delight
of the assailant who dealt out fatality tonight.

Emma Louise Pudge (14)
Prior's Field School, Godalming

Untitled

Nonchalantly, the lazy waves
Ripple on the surface.
Aluminium silver foil
Rests there, on the mighty ocean's
Silk veneer, sparkling under shimmering light,
As the sun sets.
Dismissing another day.

Rose washes through the pale blue sky
Patching the clouds. A tint of pink.
Salt air tingles my skin,
Seagulls screech above my head. Laughing.

The waves crash upon tawny sand, aggravating the petite pebbles.
They roll along the ground.
They crunch beneath my feet.

As I gaze beyond the horizon
Thoughts pervade my mind.

The wonder that is the sea.

Poppy McGrath (14)
Prior's Field School, Godalming

The Day I Got My Pony, Ronan

The vetting.
The adrenalin,
I feel scared, what if he does not pass, still no pony.
Yes, yes!
I now have a pony again,
The pony of my dreams is now mine.
We take him home
Getting him out is the exciting part,
In a field he is happily getting used to his new surroundings.

Three days later . . .

My first event on my new pony
It all goes great and at prize giving
The results are even greater,
5/6 rosettes for our first show together,
Not bad for a first time out.

Tired,
Bed is all I can think about.

Lucy Collecott (12)
Prior's Field School, Godalming

What Matters To Me?

What matters to me are my five senses,
Sight, smell, touch, hear and taste
We use them each day without thinking;
Some might say it's a waste.

For a life without sight is a life without colour,
Every day would be a great deal duller

And a life without smell, well what can I say?
I'd miss it more every single day.

Touch is the variation of soft and hard
Yes, without touch, life would be greatly marred.

Hearing, where would a life of communicating go?
It might still exist but surely rather slow?

How can I describe taste? It's like the taste of water.
It's what everything is built on, bricks and mortar.

Yes can't you see, these are the things that matter to me.

Sophie Rafter (13)
Prior's Field School, Godalming

Tips On Being Individual

Be yourself.
Embrace your personality
it's the one thing
that is truly your speciality.

If I want to say something
that others find weird, then
I pity them. Speaking your
mind is not something to be feared.

Don't follow a leader.
Take the step and leave the sheep
behind. Become your own leader
and take the leap.

If others don't appreciate
you in all your crazy glory,
then they don't deserve you.
So say bye, not sorry!

Melissa Price (14)
Prior's Field School, Godalming

Relaxing

I just want to chill and stare,
at the sky filled with clouds,
take a deep breath to smell the natural air,
packed with hope and care.
As I stare and glare I think,
about everything and everywhere,
trying to sort out my issues,
yet the natural breeze pushes me away,
away from stress and distress,
oh, I just think of relaxing,
I feel as if someone has dropped me,
dropped me in a glass of peace.

Mariam Hussein (14)
Prior's Field School, Godalming

What Matters To Me?

What matters to me?
What matters to you?
It's what matters to you, that matters to me,
Whatever you care about, matters to me.
Serious things, silly things.
All the things that interest you.
Your hobbies, are my hobbies,
Because they fascinate you.
I care about your opinion of what matters to you.
Big things, small things.
All the things in this world,
That you are curious about.
Everything in your mind,
That you find important.

Don't you get it?
You matter to me.

Yolanda Foo [13]
Prior's Field School, Godalming

What Is Love?

What is love I say?
Is love the sweet scent of roses on a summer's day?

What is love I pray?
Is love the singing and dancing, so happy and gay?

What is love I cry?
Is love the sad salty tears from someone's eye?

What is love I sigh?
Is love your heart so bitter and dry?

What is love I say?
Does the world know what love really is,
Or have we lost it in all our sins?

Maddy Simmonds [12]
Prior's Field School, Godalming

What Matters To Me

What matters to me is the summer,
The sun shining brightly all day,
Bees buzzing boldly from dawn until dusk,
And flowers arranged in amazing bouquets.

What matters to me is music,
Each song with its own unique tune,
Lyrics full of deep meanings,
Singing along with my friends until noon.

What matters to me is my sleep,
Taking me out of this world every night,
Waking up calm and refreshed,
Ready to face the new day feeling bright.

What matters to me are my friends,
We share each memory together,
They are there whenever I need them,
I know I'll remember them forever.

Elektra Georgiakakis (14)
Prior's Field School, Godalming

My Dog

I had been dreading this moment since the day I got him,
His big brown eyes stared straight into mine,
I remembered the days I used to play with him,
But they were gone,
Now his body hung limp in my arms.

I had endured this pain for so long,
I felt like my heart was being torn apart,
Between reality and fate,
I felt a teardrop trickle down my face,
I took a deep breath and cried.

His heart was beating very slowly,
His inquisitive little face peered,
Over my arm to the ground,
He was trembling with fear,
And, as I gently kissed him goodbye,
His heart led to a grinding halt and finally stopped.

Ashley Davies (12)
Prior's Field School, Godalming

Untitled

When someone you love is gone,
Your heart yearns for their presence,
The photos smile and you remember memories,
You know they will never come back.

The tears fall down from your streaming eyes,
You cry out in pain and anguish,
You are all alone, nobody hears you,
You have to learn to cope with the pain.

As the days go on the pain grows less,
You eat and sleep without then,
No one understands has much you feel,
The anger and hate of this terrible world.

They will have a place in your heart forever,
Angels within you, helping you heal the pain,
They will always be with you wherever you go.

Georgina Cave (13)
Prior's Field School, Godalming

Awakened To See Again

Every morning I doth wake
And open up my eyes,
Rejoice do I that I have sight,
Not still in world of lies.
The falsity of dreams, I think,
Do trick my waking mind,
So mirror hanging on the wall,
I gladly seek and find.
My bleary eyes awakened now
To see the world around,
Above all senses my sight I love
Above both smell and sound.
Above both smell and sound.

Anna Blades (13)
Prior's Field School, Godalming

Again

I listen as the squeak
of the zip fills the silence.
I hold my breath
while the hand rummages around,
looking for the right piece
of the multicoloured rainbow
that is my home.
We are pushed around
in a tidal wave of clutter
and then it stops.
I watch gloomily
as the ultra sharp HB pencil
is removed from the clutches
of the worn fabric again.

Molly D'Angelo (14)
Prior's Field School, Godalming

My Golden Horse

I watch my golden horse in his field,
Munching carefully on the lush green grass,
He's like a shiny reflection of a shield,
He's like shining gold brass.

He spooks, from the sound of a flapping bird,
He spins round and canters gracefully down the steep hill,
Swishing his tail like he's head of a herd,
He stops suddenly like a scratching train and remains still.

He now knows the birds are no danger,
He sets his head down and munches again,
I call to my golden angel and he knows I'm no stranger,
He does a flowing trot to my side,
Then I mount him and we walk down the lane.

Sophie Roberts (12)
Prior's Field School, Godalming

What Matters To Me

It doesn't matter if you're fat or thin.
What matters is you love your body,
Whatever skin you're in.

Some people take it to the extreme,
Eating not enough food,
Even in their dreams.

But some people just don't care,
About their weight,
And pile it on thinking it's unfair.

I don't think my body's perfect,
But I don't mind,
Even if I'm not the best human object.

Charlie Sullivan (15)
Prior's Field School, Godalming

What Matters To Me In A Friend

Trust me and I will always trust you,
Laugh with me and I will joke with you,
Care for me and I will care for you,
Be at ease and relax with me
And I will find peace with you.

Be different from me and live your own life,
For the best of friends are different at heart.

So, when I sing you can dance,
When I skip you can prance
And when I frown you can smile.

But one similarity that should always stay
Is love me and I will always love you.

Hannah Walker (12)
Prior's Field School, Godalming

The Man

Along the way
To the beautiful bay
There was a place
Where every case
Can be solved
New or old
Except for this one
Strumming a guitar
In a car
There was a man
Wearing a black coat
But no one knew his name
He could not tell
So he was thought not to be well
Until the day
He had to pay
The price of getting his way
Every day
And after that
We saw a black bat
That looked like the man
Strumming a guitar
In a car
Still no one knew his name
But he was not to blame
And there it was
The mystery because
A few years later
A big fat hater
In a van
Saw the ghost of the black man.

Katie Abson (11)
Rye St Antony School, Oxford

Terrified Thoughts

A pool of red liquid grows on the ground,
Red and blue sirens are whirling around.
It fills my head now, the pain on his face
But I must not slow down the speed of my pace.
I feel people's eyes burn into my head
And I feel right now that I'd rather be dead
Than walk on these streets where death's everywhere.
But I must meet the guys round by the store,
They'll help me, I'm sure.
My pocket feels wet - and then I remember
That what I have done will stay with me forever.
And when will I sleep?
Probably never.
The voice in my head won't stay quiet.
What happens next?
My mind is so vexed.
My stomach is screaming
And my weapon is gleaming
Red.
My boss said
To hide it under my bed.
He'll help me, I'm sure,
He knows what it's like,
He's done it before.
I'm in the gang now,
For once I'll be cool.
Splat!
What's that?
I walked in the pool.
The whirring gets louder,
They're now on the street,
My face like a sheet
And here I am.
I look like a flag -
Blood-red footsteps,
Weapon in a bag,
For I am Steph,
Lord of Death.

The cage door closes with a bang
And the voice says again,
'Why did you try to join a gang?'

Minnie Anderson (11)
Rye St Antony School, Oxford

War In The World

The war in the world . . .

Most people stay at home, not a care in the world,
To them it seems like a normal day.
But, somewhere else in the world,
Someone just had a big price to pay.

It was not their fault, doing what they were told,
They had not even a second to fight,
The story, about to unfold,
Trying for their life, trying to hold on tight.

Back over here, playing in the playground,
No idea, what has begun,
Soldiers all in a big mound,
Soldier just died, because of the last bullet gun.

A life just lost,
Yet another one soon,
Just one of the costs.
A time too soon.

We still are as oblivious now,
As what we were then,
Like it was the best day ever,
Not even a care for them.

That's what hurts the most,
Now and then,
Someone just gone,
And not a care for them . . .

Tilly O'Shea (11)
Rye St Antony School, Oxford

Deforestation Acrostic

D ire is the ring of flame
E njoyed by men as their game
F or the forest falls for their greed
O rang-utans with homes in need
R oaming where great trees are felled
E xamining where they once dwelled
S moke gradually clears to reveal
T ree stumps that will never heal
A nd profits are made in faraway lands
T he money goes to undeserving hands
I do not think this is fair
O nly men who did this, do not care
N othing is perfect in this world.

Olivia Purvis (11)
Rye St Antony School, Oxford

My Fat Cat!

Rats, bats and even gnats,
None the same as my fat cat!
I love it so much,
I can't start to explain
How it seems to entertain
By drumming and strumming on a perfect guitar
Whilst cunningly constructing a rocket powered car.
I'm not saying that it is especially bright or clever
But it seems to be able to predict the weather,
And I know this may sound awfully silly
But it appears to like the smell of lilies.
And that is the story of my beautiful cat,
Terribly clever . . . and incredibly fat!

Catherine Dorrian & Alice Mitchell (11)
Rye St Antony School, Oxford

A Town Where Olive Trees Grow

I come from a town called Nablus
In a land where the prophets roamed
A town between two mountains
Where springs and rivers flow.

The trees that grow are olives, my Sidi tells me so
As a child he used to water them and get to watch them grow
But then another army came and told us all to leave
And now I can only dream about the place our olive trees blow.

But what I have to tell you is that it isn't fair you see
For I am not allowed to visit the town my Siti and Sidi know
As time goes on and I grow old I hope we will live in peace
And I will get to visit the place I long to go.

Iman Abdel-Haq (11)
Rye St Antony School, Oxford

Thoughts On Racism

You don't belong here.
You look different.
I don't want to have anything to do with you.

Why are they looking at me that way?
I'm just another human,
Not an exhibit in a museum.
I feel love and hate, joy and sorrow, hurt and pleasure.
Why am I different?
The only thing that separates us is my skin.

Ignorance is not bliss
Stop racism.

Lucy Ramsden (11)
Rye St Antony School, Oxford

The Animals Lover

My animals live with me in my mind.
I love to lie down and play.
I take them on a walk.
I go cantering on them.
I love it in the countryside to walk.
Make dens.
Climb trees.
I love them all very much.
They impress me because they do new tricks.
They inspire me.
I wish they could be with me in real life.

Sarah Horsfall (12)
Rye St Antony School, Oxford

Home Alone

Scary thoughts whirl in my head
Any moment soon I swear I would be dead
I try to think of anything else
But being home alone
It's the scariest thing of all.

Hearing the creaking floorboards
And the howling of the wolves
Strange sounds
And the knocking on the door.

Seeing the strange shapes
And continuous knocking
The chair in the corner
Has just started rocking.

Wait a minute
How could I forget?
Tonight is Halloween
So why am I at home?

Vienna Sheridan (11)
St Bernadette's Catholic Secondary School, Bristol

Granny Slam

A fight declared between two grannies,
Fighting it out for the granny slam title.
Super Nanny and Dynamite Nanny,
The best start is so vital.
Ding, ding! the bell goes.
Super Nanny throws her slippers off her toes
And hits her opponent on the nose.
Dynamite Nanny throws her needles through the air,
Hits Super Nanny and she shouts, 'It's not fair!'

Round 2 going to start, the match still so close,
The Super Nanny's false teeth fall out
And the entire crowd moan, 'Gross!'
30 seconds left of Round 2,
All the crowd biting their fingernails,
Who will win?
Dynamite Nanny uses her strength,
Picks up Super Nanny and throws her in the bin.
Super Nanny stands up in disgust,
All over her is rotten food,
Super Nanny walks over to Dynamite Nanny,
She punches her, it changes her mood.

Final round, the score's drawed,
Dynamite Nanny gets up, all the crowd roar and applaud,
Super Nanny gets up,
Both nannies walk to each other,
Face to face they stay,
Then suddenly both nannies fall down,
Now that's where they'll stay.

Taylor Channing (12)
St Bernadette's Catholic Secondary School, Bristol

The Treasure Of My Heart

You rewire my mind to know we're all beautiful
That is something that we can't deny
You put us up from being down to the best of times
That is why you are my treasure of my heart

You just don't know what you mean to me
You never let me down
You're like an angel sent from above
Also when we need you, you shower me with love

When you're there we don't ever cry a single tear
You chase away my terror
You have given me a life I will love
You should always appreciate what I have

It's even better every time you smile
It's also so magical
You bring back all the faith in the world
And now my dream has come true

Now I have found what I am looking for
It's you and your love and nothing more
Cos you have given me this feeling
In my life something I've never felt before

I wish I could talk forever until the world is over
But we might run out of words to say
So when we do I will always end with the line you already know
'I love you' more than what I could show.

Monica Elsworth (12)
St Bernadette's Catholic Secondary School, Bristol

One Step

I see a person standing there,
His face is blank but his eyes are cold,
No emotion on his face, no feelings in his heart,
Hands in pockets, eyes to the ground,

Darkness all around me, closing in,
His eyes begin to rise as the sun begins to fall,
My heart begins to sink, deeper and deeper,
One step forwards he moves,
My arms begin to dangle,
Paralysed I feel, motionless I am,

One step more,
His face shows clearer, his evil smirk,
His coal black eyes piercing through me,
He grabs me,
With a painful grasp around my arms,
He shakes me,

I awake,
My eyes widen,
I see a room, a dark room, my room,
Night still passing,
It was all a dream,
Or shall I say a nightmare.

Georgia Ponting (13)
St Bernadette's Catholic Secondary School, Bristol

Likes/Dislikes

Football, baseball and netball,
I hate them all,
Dogs, cats and bats,
I like them all especially rats,
Bonfire Night, Halloween and Coke,
My mum thinks they're all a big hoax.

Paige Coxon (121)
St Bernadette's Catholic Secondary School, Bristol

True Love

Love at first sight is a myth, a legend,
A load of rubbish you know;
At least that's what I used to think,
Before I met Romeo.

It was hot, and boring, my heart was pounding,
And I was feeling faint;
I rested against the corridor wall,
To find I was touching wet paint.

I couldn't believe the luck I was having,
It surely can't get any worse;
And at that minute I fell to the ground,
Why's it always after saying that curse?

I woke with a start, surrounded by people,
I felt I was part of the zoo;
And that's when I saw him, tall, dark and handsome,
I felt like buttery goo!

And it's been like that ever since that day,
So I think I should let you all know;
That love at first sight's not a myth, nor a legend,
You'll see when you meet Romeo!

Frances Bridgman (11)
St Bernadette's Catholic Secondary School, Bristol

Untitled

Terror
Is like a hiding turtle
Moving slow,
Trying to get away
On the sandy beach floor
In terror of the humans
Who want to eat her.

Sean Noonan (12)
St Bernadette's Catholic Secondary School, Bristol

150

California

To you it's a haze,
But to me a lovely place.

People having fun,
In the boiling hot sun.

Two weeks of heaven,
Always beats Devon.

California's the place to go,
When you're feeling low.

Every day something to do,
According to Sue.

Roller coasters day one,
Competitions done.

Day two relax,
Said Max.

Days three to fourteen,
Shop until you drop.

Alice O'Farrell (12)
St Bernadette's Catholic Secondary School, Bristol

Thunder And Lightning

It was a stormy night
Out at sea, with nothing but a light,
The old man and his son were brave,
While all hid in a cave
Then . . . *boom!*
The thunder and lightning hit the sea,
He was as light as a pea,
He was hurled in the air . . .
Seconds passed, he never came back,
So it was his last thunder and lightning at sea.

Calum Rogers (12)
St Bernadette's Catholic Secondary School, Bristol

Netball

As soon as the whistle blows
That is when everyone goes
To the centre third to catch
The ball but remember you have to snatch.

If you catch the ball remember
To pass it to the shoot or centre
And run to the top of the court
But don't let them catch you short.

If the ball makes it to the circle
Remember to shoot and try your best
If not at all
All is wasted.

Now we scored
We're winning 1-0
Keep playing excellently
We'll have it in the bag.

Amelia Bettesworth (11)
St Bernadette's Catholic Secondary School, Bristol

Daddy Cool

My daddy is so cool
He lets me play basketball
I don't usually do this but I think it's quite cool
Me and my daddy, we go to the pool
And have a little cool off
My daddy is so cool, he is the best on April Fools
Me and my daddy, well what I can I say
I just think he's cool
He buys me treats, gives me money
He is just so cool
Me and my daddy sometimes have a paddy
But then we are both cool!

Alexandra Joan Connell (12)
St Bernadette's Catholic Secondary School, Bristol

Halloween

It was a dark and eerie night,
Under the pale glow of the candlelight.
Hungry children swarm the streets,
Searching eagerly for some tasty treats.

Perhaps they're children, perhaps not,
Or maybe they're zombies - dead flesh and rot.
Disguised in a mask and hooded cloak,
Some hide with eggs near windows they broke.

Mischief and mayhem is none the less,
As ghouls and villains create a mess.
Preying on victims who are weak and frail,
The Devil lurks, not leaving a trail.

The full moon shone so bright,
Those werewolves howled with all their might.
Sending those monsters running with fear,
They won't be back for another year!

Kira Thomas [11]
St Bernadette's Catholic Secondary School, Bristol

Waiting

I'm here waiting in the cold winter night.

I saw the lamp post shine so bright.
I'm sitting on the edge of a fountain with nothing to do.
I'm just here waiting for you.
My eye starts to tear up like the first drop of rain.
How long was I here?
Well for me it feels like a year.
Suddenly it starts to snow
So now I have to go
But I will say no
Because I will stay here waiting for you.

Jerlen Pangilinan [13]
St Bernadette's Catholic Secondary School, Bristol

Haikus

Haikus
First five syllables
Now put seven syllables
Now put five again.

Night
Night is utter black
Stars and the moon shine brightly
The day is coming.

School
School is just a waste
What is the point in learning?
Just let kids go home.

Flight
Flight is beautiful
Birds and planes soar above clouds
I wish I could fly.

Frederick Pearce [12]
St Bernadette's Catholic Secondary School, Bristol

Sunday Football

I'm up and ready in my dad's car,
Off to football, we haven't got far,
We're there in no time and ready to start,
I'm so excited, I can feel the beat of my heart,
The whistle blows, the game is on,
We have several chances to lead,
But alas they have gone,
We have a break and time to reflect,
As soon as we restart we hit the net,
That's the score, the game ends,
As I'm holding the match ball with my friends.

Josh McQuaid [11]
St Bernadette's Catholic Secondary School, Bristol

My Sister

My sister is a funny girl, she wears loads of pears,
Running around, mad.
She hates boys with their little toys
Thinking they're so hard but they're as tough as a card.

She loves her sister
But she runs around after her like a twister,
Buying her new clothes 'cause she can't afford the money
Because she spends it all on her tummy.

Her mother who spends all day driving her car
Going up to the bar, having a drink or two.
Her mother tries to do stuff with her like going to the zoo
But when they get there all she wants to do is go to the loo.

So that is the story of my sister Jenny,
My aunty calls her a little penny,
So I'll see you soon at the top of the moon.

Lewis Rogers (11)
St Bernadette's Catholic Secondary School, Bristol

My Family

My sister's a pain,
Well it is a gain.
I boss her about,
She gives me a pout!

My mum's a save,
She gives me a wave.
She cannot resist,
She gives me a lift!

That just leaves me,
Now to see
What I can write,
I'm not so bright!

Neve McDonnell (11)
St Bernadette's Catholic Secondary School, Bristol

The Wild Horses

They gallop across the open plains
as free as the wind
that combs through their manes.
They race and race
a blur of many colours
never ever to break their pace.
They are as free as they want to be
their untamed souls
never destined to carry you and me.
They have no barn or stable as their home
nothing they can call their own
just the land in which they roam.
They are wild and meant to be
no one to calm those hearts of fire
for their home is land where they can be free.

Ellie Daly (13)
St Bernadette's Catholic Secondary School, Bristol

Shadow Man

Shadow Man comes in the night
Shadow Man gives you a fright

Shadow Man copies every move
Wherever you go there's no place for escaping
Because he's there

But all Shadow Man really wants
Is to have a friend
So next time you see him
Don't shout or scream
Just say hello

But be careful
Because he might steal your shadow!

Lauryn Duffy (11)
St Bernadette's Catholic Secondary School, Bristol

Fear

Fear,
Is a terrifying monster,
Sneaking up to his vulnerable victims,
In a dark scary room
To scare you to death.
Excitement,
Is a jumping kangaroo,
Bouncing around just for fun,
On the dry grassy savannah,
To thrill you.
Pride,
Is a mighty lion,
Slowly creeping up to his unfortunate prey,
In the leafy closed jungle,
To hunt for his living.

Safiyyah Abdul-Karim [12]
St Bernadette's Catholic Secondary School, Bristol

Happy Halloween

It was a dark and spooky night,
My torch was beaming light.
My heart beat once, twice, three times,
And heard all the whines.
The floorboard creaked,
The children were freaked.

Perhaps they are not children,
Argh!
The outside cold,
The kidnappers bold.

The trees, swaying side to side,
I tried to hide.

Millie Meacham [11]
St Bernadette's Catholic Secondary School, Bristol

Him <3

I might die, when I forget how to breathe,
You get closer and there's nowhere in this world I'd rather be.
Time starts like everything around me is frozen
And nothing matters but these few moments,
When you open my mind to things I've never seen.

Past loves, they never got very far,
Wall's up, make sure I guarded my heart.
I promised I wouldn't do this till I knew it was right for me.
But no one, no guy that I'd met before could make me
Feel so right and secure.

I've never felt anything like this,
You're making me open up,
No point in trying to fight this,
It kinda feels like it's love.

Storm Hanks [13]
St Bernadette's Catholic Secondary School, Bristol

My Hobbies

My favourite sport is swimming
I also like winning

The Wii's really fun
I play it with my mum

The laptop has lots of games
I also like it when it rains

Bowling is funny
The milkshake is runny

The trampoline's probably the best.

Saul Pitter [12]
St Bernadette's Catholic Secondary School, Bristol

My Shadow

When I am sad my shadow is like a lost soul,
Just walking and walking,
Walking straight not moving,
Only its hair flies in the wind,
And the repeated sway of its arms.

When the weather is dull,
I have no shadow,
I feel alone,
Gloomy, damp and no breeze,
Not even the wind is there to talk to me.

When I'm my shadow plays with me,
Runs with me,
Jumps higher than me.
When I'm happy, I'm not alone.

Shani Avery (12)
St Bernadette's Catholic Secondary School, Bristol

I Like/Don't Like

I don't like poems
I don't like rhyme
I don't like getting homework all the time

I like rugby
I like sport
I like hanging out in the tennis court

I didn't want to do this poem
I will read it in front of a crowd
Because I am proud.

Michael Morgan (11)
St Bernadette's Catholic Secondary School, Bristol

Football

F ootball is a game of skill
O ur team will win
O ut in a football stadium
T he whistle goes
B ut it's a free-kick in the tenth minute
A nd someone scores a goal
L oads of people cheering for me
L ots of supporters.

Jeffrey Grimes (11)
St Bernadette's Catholic Secondary School, Bristol

Gloom!

Gloom!
He is a lonely wolf,
Wailing, crying out,
He has no family,
He is the only one,
He is on his own,
He is the wolf.

Ellie Marie Hodges (12)
St Bernadette's Catholic Secondary School, Bristol

The Pumpkin

Orange like a tiger lily.
Round like the Earth.
Sweet like chocolate.
Heavy like an elephant.
The pumpkin.

Anna Korba (13)
St Bernadette's Catholic Secondary School, Bristol

Sadness

Sadness is a tired lion
Long tail drooped to the floor
In the hot plains of Africa
Wishing it was in the shade
By a cool nice river.

Isaac Parker (12)
St Bernadette's Catholic Secondary School, Bristol

The Girl From Bury

There was a girl from Bury who fell over,
And said, 'Help me in a hurry!'
She fell on her knee, 'Please, please help me!'
Only to find the girl from Bury
Had slipped on some curry.

Regan Sollars (12)
St Bernadette's Catholic Secondary School, Bristol

Mum

Mum, you're always there for me,
In my life you're the special key,
To live without you,
It is hard to think too,
Whenever I'd turn round,
You'd always be there standing your ground,
Now I'm growing older,
You don't have to look over your shoulder,
I'll always be buried in your heart,
Forever long we will never part.

Rebecca Coolahan (12)
St Paul's Catholic College, Sunbury on Thames

Death At Hand

By day these men ask nothing and obey;
They eat their bread behind a heap of stones;
Hardship and violence grow an easy way,
Winter is like a girl within their bones.

They learn the gambits of the soul,
Think lightly of the themes of life and death,
All mortal anguish shrunk into an ache
Too nagging to be worth the catch of breath.

Sharing life's iron rations, marching light,
Enduring to the end the early cold,
The emptiness of noon, the void of night
I whose black market they are bought and sold;
They take their silent stations for the fight
Rum's holy unction makes the dubious bold.

Ryan Harris Conyard (11)
St Paul's Catholic College, Sunbury on Thames

Dancing With Stars And The Moon

I look at the sky and I wonder
can stars really dance together.
I just wait a few seconds to see,
stars start twinkling at me.

The moon shines like she is a silver plate
and reflects at the River Thames.
The sky is metallic blue
so I ask, 'What am I supposed to do?'

I look at the moon again,
could it be bigger than Big Ben?
If the moon is Earth's son how come
everything was created and done?

William Souza (11)
St Paul's Catholic College, Sunbury on Thames

Summertime!

In
The hot
Summertime
The birds come out
Singing in the bright
Sun with their sweet
Voices. The
Grass is
Green.

Alexandra Wilson (11)
St Paul's Catholic College, Sunbury on Thames

The Rain

There's holes in the sky,
To let rain in,
But the holes are small,
That's why rain's thin.

Rebecca McGovern (12)
St Paul's Catholic College, Sunbury on Thames

In My Life I Need

In my life I need,
In my life I need my family, friends and my faithful dog,
In my life I need food, drink and don't forget the chips,
In my life I need jeans, T-shirt and my smelly socks,
In my life I need shops, town and really big cities,
I am,
I am no one without all these things.

Joshua Arnell (13)
The Gregg School, Southampton

Night Ride

Swerve down to the drive,
3,000 miles away till we will soon arrive,
Clutch the handle bars,
Then weaving between the cars,
We roar away,
Leaving the cars to beat us another day,

Wind rushing on my face,
Could I be in a better place?

Whizz on and on,
Home is long since gone,
Leaving behind the teachers, who bark and bite,
Pulling back we halt at the lights,
Stuck between lorry and car,
Feeling intimidated and bizarre,

Wind rushing on my face,
Could I be in a better place?

Adrenaline hurries through my bones,
Skidding around traffic cones,
A stride my monster I shiver,
As I watch the glowing river,
Silver helmet matched with bike,
The twisting road ahead of me that all the bikers like,

Wind rushing on my face,
Could I be in a better place?

Then we're a silver streak,
Next to the blue of the creek,
If I were in control,
We would be chased by all the officers on patrol,
Wishing to go even faster,
Exhausts blaring like a super blaster,

Wind rushing on my face,
Could I be in a better place?

When I'm lying in the dark I dream,
Of riding my speed machine,
I'd whizz through the darkness just a streak,

Passing every expensive boutique,
Mum and Dad would be yelling slow down,
I'd just go faster, helmet like a crown,
Zooming away into the night,
My heart taking flight,

Smile spreads on my face,
I wish I was in my favourite place.

Felicity Heath (11)
The Gregg School, Southampton

Healthy Eating

It sits there on a vast white snow
My one way ticket to dessert
The one problem before the train leaves
It stares at me through red puffy eyes
Its brains slime over the plate
I slouch and slump on my chair

Jessie comes in, her tail up high, expectant
My saviour with a lolling tongue, my true best friend
A plan hatches like a newborn chick
Unsteady on its feet
Mother's back is turned

Quickly the red mess slumps onto the floor
Come here girl eat the disaster
She trots over, she sniffs, she licks
She runs off with her tail between her legs
My hope running off with her

It comes to this
He has been squashed under my knife
Pushed around my plate trying to get smaller
Healthy eating is a struggle
When even the dog won't eat my tomato
Some friend she turned out to be.

Victoria Regan (13)
The Gregg School, Southampton

You Can't Take The Sky From Me

Stars, blazing sparks,
Lighting up our darkest hour,
All alone in the night.

Huge, brilliant balls,
Of burning gas,
Like millions of fireflies in the dark.

Blackness,
Filling every space between,
These giant beacons of fire.

Balls of rock,
Racing around,
Springing awe and wonder, even in the most unlikely of places.

Earth, our home,
But such a small particle,
Concealed in a shadow of the vast galaxy.

Since the dawn of civilisation,
We looked at the moon,
We have gazed and thought

Is it impossible?
Are we just too small, too insignificant to break into the night?
No, nothing is truly impossible, only on the surface.

We send up rockets,
Imagine ships that scale space,
Continuing to strive to see, to know, to explore.

It is the destiny of Man,
Born under a star
And he will not rest until he is among them?

Fire from within,
A surging force, a power so intense,
It alone will carry him to the stars.

'Burn the land
And boil the sea,
But you can't take the sky from me'.

Ross Castle (14)
The Gregg School, Southampton

My Family

I have a brother called Charlie,
Who seems to have a habit,
Of eating lots of tea,
I'm scared he might eat me.

I have a mum called Jacqueline,
Who seems to have a habit,
Of cooking something yummy,
I'm scared she might cook me.

I have a sister called Jenna,
Who seems to have a habit,
Of hiding all her mess,
I'm scared she might hide me.

I have a dad called Martin,
He seems to have a habit,
Of burying the seeds,
I'm scared he might bury me.

I am called Rebecca,
I seem to have a habit,
Of liking my family,
They are all perfect for me!

Rebecca Fogden (11)
The Gregg School, Southampton

What Matters To Me?

What matters to me?
Is it your favourite toy,
That you never let go?
Could it be a pet,
That always makes you happy?

What matters to you?
Is it a holiday that you had,
That always makes you smile?
Could it be food,
Like a chocolate that you can't live without?

What matters to you?
Is it a song, that brings back memories?
Could it be a film,
That you watch every Christmas with family?

What matters to you?
Is it a lovely glass of wine,
After a hard day's work
Or a book that your parents read to you at night?

What matters to you?
Friends and family,
Being there when you need them?
Could it be a smell,
That takes you back?

What matters to you?
The sound of rain,
Or just the fact the sun has come out?
Could it be a rainbow,
Brightening the sky?

Do you have a special way of doing things,
That only you know how?
Or annoying little habits,
That make everyone laugh?
I know what matters to me
My bed!

Tabitha Hunt (13)
The Gregg School, Southampton

What Was Going On?

Young and innocent
Tickling and giggling
Saying I love you
What was going on?

Going to see you
Crying at the bedside
Trying to be strong
What was going on?

Then it happened
He was gone
Never to be seen again
What was going on?

I was happy
When he was here
Now I think back
What was going on?

Now I remember
All the happy memories
I will never forget you because
I love you!

Olivia Douglas (13)
The Gregg School, Southampton

Family

Lazy Dad sleeping when he has a chance,
Sitting in front of the TV watching football,
Waiting for his team to get the ball,
Going to work every morning, always late,
But they're just dads, nothing we can do.

Working Mum trying too hard,
Cooking the food, cleaning house, all too hard,
Getting you ready for school,
Making your packed lunch, waking you up,
But they're just mums, nothing we can do.

Annoying siblings touching all your stuff,
Showing off, proving that they're better when they're actually not,
Thinking that they're better at everything, always thinking wrong,
Jealous at everything you're good at, always acting wrong,
But they're just siblings, nothing we can do.

Amazing me, the best member of the family,
Good at everything, no one else better than me,
Always with great ideas that no one else can think of,
Getting to choose what you want for your birthday,
No one better than me, I'm just amazing but that's just me,
Nothing we can do.

Fantastic family put together, all works out,
The lazy one, the trying one, the annoying one, the amazing one,
Lots of highs and lows with family,
Just like your friends, always cheering you on and supporting you,
But that's just family, nothing we can do.

Arman Shabgard (12)
The Gregg School, Southampton

What War Is

War is a sickness
War is the dark
War is the rhythm
Of the orders they bark

War isn't hope
War isn't love
War isn't the freedom
Of that snowy white dove

War is hatred
War is greed
War is separation
By colour and creed

War isn't bright
War isn't funny
War isn't fragrant
Or sweet like honey

War is dying
War is pain
War is losing
Again and again

This is what war was
This war was hers; this war was his
This is what war will forever be
Because this war
Is what war is.

Jennifer Burnage (14)
The Gregg School, Southampton

The iPod Disco

Through all of those tedious trips,
Whether it's rain or sun
Those lyrics are streaming out of my lips
And I couldn't be having more fun,
Yet I am forgetful
That I am the only one who can hear
And I wonder why nobody else
Is singing along with me,
It's as if a magician
Has made them all disappear
And left me in one-man disco
Of blissful glee,
But then I begin to see
All the colours of the spectrum together,
With everybody suddenly shimmying around
As if there's no tomorrow,
Shapes are flying all around
Making me feel as light as a feather
And all I need
Are some funky disco boots to borrow
With a few retro beats to groove to,
Then we can all shimmy simultaneously together,
With the flashing lights running through my hair
As if they were disco-style shampoo,
Nobody can ever restrict my euphoria with a tether,
Yes, my iPod really does have the power
To make me feel all of this . . .

Euan Anderson (15)
The Gregg School, Southampton

Trust

I was sitting in a pushchair
On a hot, hot beach.
I could see the sea,
But I couldn't touch it.
That was me then.

I was sitting in the sand.
Sand sieving through my fingers.
I could see the sea,
But I couldn't touch it.
That was me then.

I was running on the beach.
Paddling in the sea.
Jumping in the waves.
Looking bemused at a snorkel.
That was me then.

I was snorkelling in the sea.
Sketchy about my snorkel.
Bobbing on the waves
In hip-height of water.
That was me then.

I am swimming in the sea.
Take a few deep breaths
And dive down a couple of metres.
Swimming among the fish.
This is Jamie Bushnell.

Jamie Bushnell (14)
The Gregg School, Southampton

The Mark On The Wall!

It's big and blotchy,
Black and blue
And very, very big,
It's a large fat circle,
With a tint of pink
And a little bit of purple,
I do not like it,
The mark on our wall,
It bothers me a lot,
But most of all,
I hate it when
The atmosphere's hot,
As I'm annoyed
At everyone and everything
Around me,
Especially this big mark,
As it's not clear to anyone else,
It's annoying and disruptive,
My mummy will just look at it and say,
'It's gorgeous dear,'
And my daddy will just say,
'It's pretty just right here,'
And then they'll say,
'I love our brand new painting on the wall,'
And I'll just say,
'I hate it; I hope that it will fall!'

Charlotte Millman (12)
The Gregg School, Southampton

Outside

Outside there is grass gleaming,
Flowers blooming and squirrels gathering,
Laughing, playing, jumping up and down,
Sadness has gone, happiness has come,
Darkness going,
Sunshine coming.

Outside there are trees swaying,
Benches lining up like soldiers,
Leaves falling, autumn coming silently,
Clouds moving slowly,
Summer's end,
Around the bend.

Outside there are planes soaring,
Vapour trail appearing,
Distant air ports waiting for touchdown,
Stations communicating swiftly,
Goodbye sun,
Hello moon.

Thomas Captain (11)
The Gregg School, Southampton

My Balloon

My brother once came into my room,
Luckily he didn't burst my balloon,
In fact he broke my cocoon,
Which was next to the loo,
Maybe one day my brother will grow up,
But hopefully he will not pop,
In fact one day he will probably flop,
But not so that my balloon will blow up,
Maybe he will even kill my rabbit,
As he likes to poke him as a habit.

George Bareham (11)
The Gregg School, Southampton

Autumn

In autumn,
The trees come alive,
Apples, the king of fruits,
Pears, the queen of fruits,
They are gathered in,
Tons at a time.

Each one,
Completely individual,
Coxes,
Conference,
Comice.

And then,
The supermarkets,
Obsessed with the shine and finish,
Polish them to death
To get the perfect sheen,
In doing so,
Destroy the whole fruit.

Andrew Heath [13]
The Gregg School, Southampton

The Sunset

The sun,
Is dying as
The darkness gains on it,
The sun gives all its energy,
Then dies.

Tara Norris [13]
The Gregg School, Southampton

Horse

She gallops to the pounding pulse of drums in her heart
If I let her free
I am lost in darkness
She makes a simple field look truly stunning
Horses fly without wings
And fight without swords
And when we ride a horse we borrow freedom
There's a wild whisper in the wind
Calling out your name
Like a long-lost friend
Walking into the sunset on a late night in summertime
We have a partnership
That will never be lost
You can tame down a horse
But you will never break its spirit
I love you horse
My friend.

Claire Humby (13)
The Gregg School, Southampton

TV

TV,
All that matters to me is TV,
A big comfy chair,
Exciting new episodes
And all I do is stare.

Sitting with my family,
Bag of crisps for me to enjoy,
Drinking my favourite drink,
Waiting for the adverts to end,
Quizzes that make me think,

That's why TV matters to me.

William Gray (12)
The Gregg School, Southampton

The Smell Of Books

The smell of books,
What a wonderful smell!
They all smell different as well!

New books are crisp,
The pages turn well
But a bit overwhelming is this smell!

Plastic books remind me of hard days at school,
Long maths lessons, I don't miss it!
They smell of dollies I used to get at Christmas.

But my favourite of all has to be old,
All the classics by Dickens and Austen,
Their smell is near gone, just misting.

So when I go shopping with all my friends,
They walk to perfume -
And I follow, or so they assume!

Amber Holland [12]
The Gregg School, Southampton

My Family

My family
My family are kind
My family care
Whenever I need them my family are there
My family are quiet
My family yell
But most of the time we get on so well
My sister is bossy
But not all the time
I am so glad this family is mine
My family.

Alexander Chessell [12]
The Gregg School, Southampton

What Is Love?

What is love?
Is it a game?
A feeling, a word or a name?

Love is a feeling
A feeling inside
A feeling that most people cannot hide.

Love is a word
Taken for granted
A word that is whispered, shouted or chanted.

Love is a name
With four letters only
Sometimes it's even considered holy.

Love is a game
Of choice and fate
Only you can find your true soulmate.

Charlotte Bull [14]
The Gregg School, Southampton

How Scary The Darkness Is

Night-time
Street lamps flicker
No one is outside now
A rustling in the distance
A scream.

Greg Anderson [13]
The Gregg School, Southampton

Family

A twinkling, shining star gleams brighter than all the rest.
This is like my family. To me they are the best.

A gentle flowing river that runs down to the sea.
Always there and never stops, that's my mum to me.

The sea is calm and peaceful but always entertaining
Like Dad who is hilarious, unless he is complaining.

Cute and cheeky monkeys who only want to play
Like my brother, Riccardo, who does football every day.

Delicate and fragrant cherry blossom on a tree
That's my Nonna Paula who is very close to me.

Tall trees in my garden, standing strong and true
Just like my two grandads, who have humour through and through.

I love my family dearly, and a message to them from me,
You're kind, helpful and caring, you're the perfect family.

Sophie Barnard (11)
The Gregg School, Southampton

Dexter, My Dog

You are my soft, playful little dog,
My glowing light in the fog,
You are my life in a battlefield,
My sword, my armour, my shield.

You are my place to escape reality,
My freedom, kingdom and city.
You are my icing on a bun,
My joy, excitement and fun.

You are my everlasting friend,
My buddy, someone I cannot comprehend.
You are my gravity, that keeps me on this Earth,
You are my everything, life, soul and worth.

Dominick Levoi (14)
The Gregg School, Southampton

Shoes

Walking down the street
On my owner's feet,
A lovely little lady with a hip hop beat.

Sometimes I am tall,
Sometimes I am small,
Whenever my owner needs me
I am always on call.

The world is but a step away
Together we explore the way,
Until one day she walks no more
I rest alone by the door.

Now I am lost without my sole.
One day we'll meet again?
Perhaps this will be my goal
To take a sweet and heavenly stroll.

Addison Vincent (12)
The Gregg School, Southampton

Love And War

The tranquillity of it
The way it makes you feel that you're lighter than a cloud
The way it blocks out everything that doesn't matter
You never want it to end

The terror of it
The way it can take loved ones forever
The way it torments you in every step it takes
You pray for it to end

Why won't it stay?
Why does it return without authority?
So many questions without any answers
The only thing you have left is pain . . .

Joe D'Souza (14)
The Gregg School, Southampton

Morning, Midday And Midnight

Morning,
How I hate it
Getting up so early.
One thing I always want to do
Lie in.

Midday,
How the sun shines
And you can hear the birds singing.
Everyone is having fun. Jolly
Summer.

Midnight,
All you can hear
Is the gentle wind blowing
And you can see nothing at all but
Darkness.

Emma Birch (13)
The Gregg School, Southampton

Outside

Outside there are lots and lots of trees,
Birds flying, butterflies dying,
I'm crying,
Planes flying.

Vapour trail in the sky,
Why can't I learn to fly?
Clouds moving,
Cows mooing.

Outside birds flying high,
Squirrels go nuts over nuts,
They can't lie,
Neither can I.

James Atkinson (11)
The Gregg School, Southampton

Outside!

Outside there are birds tweeting,
There are trees that stand so tall,
Wind blowing calmly,
Plants shooting,
Trees rooting.

Outside there are leaves weaving in and out of wood,
There are butterflies flying above me,
Vapour trails from planes,
Clouds whisping away,
Diamond grass, beautiful day.

Outside there's the sun in my face,
There are squirrels eating acorns off the tree,
Autumn leaves on the grass blowing away,
Red leaves,
Coloured leaves.

Lauren Scappaticci (11)
The Gregg School, Southampton

The Morning

Why, God?
It's so comfy
Mum rudely awakens me
So I snap and bellow loudly
No school!

Nathan Thomas (13)
The Gregg School, Southampton

Who Likes Cheese?

I like it, he likes it,
She likes it too.

The soft, creamy goodness,
Makes me luminous,
With a glass of red wine,
Right by my side.
I feel quite at home,
With my cheese!

I like, he likes it,
She likes it too.

Packed in my lunch already for school,
All my friends are jealous so I must be cool.
I love all the cheesy string together,
Now I'll know I'll love my cheese forever.

Holly Mumford (12)
The Gregg School, Southampton

Helicopter Rescue

The alarm goes off
In the rescue station
A boat in distress.
The waves are huge
And there's no way out.

Rotor blades are spinning
And up goes the rescue team.
The wind is strong
But they keep on going.

Down goes the winch
To pick up the people,
Frightened and shivering.
It's all in a day's work.

Andrew Pimm (11)
The Gregg School, Southampton

Paradox

A raven watches the humans go by,
A simple life, no worries, problems, nothing.
But people, they must do these things, for it
Is in their nature to question; indeed,
Is it that all ravens are black? Or what of
Heterology and exceptions and
Oh so much more the mind must ponder, never
To be as simple as a raven's mind.

Meanwhile, a man, he walks alone, in night,
In day, who knows he knows nothing at all.
In need of that which cannot be found then,
Or ever, for it can't be found in need.
To be as free and as naïve as ravens,
A blessing on mankind that would be indeed.

Ben Woodley (12)
The Gregg School, Southampton

Outside

Outside there are trees blowing in the gentle breeze.
The sun is glistening on the leaves of the trees.
Squirrels dancing.

Outside there are fluffy white clouds
That look like balls of candyfloss.
The birds are twirling in the sunlight
Like they are having a good day.
Birds singing.

Outside there are seeds waiting to become trees
And bushes growing bigger and bigger.
In time trees will become older and older
Then eventually they will die.
Trees glistening.

Wyatt Brennan (11)
The Gregg School, Southampton

My Ideal Home

My ideal home,
Is regularly shown
On TV,
People watching on their settees.

Because,
It is the home
Of rugby,
Twickenham Rugby Ground,
Found
In 1910.

It will have many hen nights
And also, many stag nights,
But mainly,
Much rugby,
Where England
Lost to Scotland,
At the first ever game.

Roman Malin (13)
The Matthew Arnold School, Staines

Speed

Some people say that speed is a demon;
But I feel as if it's a sense of freedom.

It's not just in a car,
That speed will take you far,
But on bikes and planes
And even fast trains.

It's all around us, it takes us through the day,
Without speed there is no delay.

Jay Simpson (14)
The Matthew Arnold School, Staines

When You Smile

When you smile, the whole world changes.
The winter trees start to blossom
And the rose bush rearranges.

The sun comes out from the gloomy sky
And the sound of calm waves
Can be heard nearby.

The baby birds start to fly,
For the first time, just for a try.

When you smile, all my fears get washed away
And replaced by joy that I get on New Year's Day.

Your smile means so much to me,
So you ought to know, before you go down,
On one knee!

Mona Gholami (13)
The Matthew Arnold School, Staines

My Ideal Home

I'm just like you
I'm homeless too
I wish all my dreams
Would just come true

I need beds and chairs
What type? Who cares?
With entertainment and food
Or a visit to Bude

I need make-up and hair bits
Or a visit to the air pits
I need an environment that's safe
Or a visit to my nan's place

I need to be me, me, me!

Debbie Hawthorn (11)
The Matthew Arnold School, Staines

Home

Home is like a little box
Stuffed with all my memories.
Home is a place where I
Can actually be me.

Home is where my loved ones are
And can never go away.
Home smells like cooking
A lovely smell that never ends.

Home's like a tree that
Keeps blossoming every day.
Home is so wonderful
I always want to stay
Or do I . . . ?

Anesha Tarapdar
The Matthew Arnold School, Staines

My Ideal Home

My ideal home would probably be,
Jumping and laughing
And playing on my PlayStation 3.

I would love to have my own TV,
Maybe 40
Or even 50!

I would love to have my dog with me,
His name would be Badger or even Scruffy!

My mobile phone to text my friends
And invite them over to play,
Jumping about like mad
And hoping they will stay all day!

Lauren Clarey (11)
The Matthew Arnold School, Staines

My Ideal Home

A home is where you feel safe,
A home is where you feel proud and brave,
It holds all your memories,
And those memories should remain.

A home can bring you hope,
A home can keep you warm and dry,
It helps you have confidence,
When all else dies.

A home is where your family is,
A home is where you can relax.
It helps you be yourself,
This is my ideal house!

Josie Evans (12)
The Matthew Arnold School, Staines

Home Sweet Home

Home sweet home is the place for me,
I'd eat sweets all day and have chocolate for tea.
I'll do what I want, whenever I feel,
Not go to sleep until I feel ill.

Icing walls and cupcake seats,
A dazzling sofa to rest my feet.
Liquorice bed and pretty pink walls,
To not live here you would be a fool.

A garden so green, with grass growing lots,
Sticky red bugs made from humbugs and tots.
I really love my dream home,
I could build it myself, the door out of foam.

Lauren Farrell (11) & Charlotte Evans
The Matthew Arnold School, Staines

My Ideal Home

Look at my house, my house is amazing
Have a look, it's amazing!

Home is where I play my PS3
And where I play with my brother.
Home is where I do my homework.
Home is where I live.
Home is where I sleep.

 H ome is where I live.
 O oo I love my home.
 M y home is where my family are.
 E very day I am at my home.

Tom Brock
The Matthew Arnold School, Staines

My Ideal Home

I could just wish for amazing things,
Like my house flying on enormous wings,
Or filled with jelly right to the top,
So I can fill my belly and not have to stop!

The problem is that will never happen
So for those ideas I will have to put a cap on,
But I am sure my ideal home would be
What it is right now, it's perfect to me.

Maisie Marshall (12)
The Matthew Arnold School, Staines

Home - My Ideal Home

Home is where my family is,
Home is where I sleep,
Home is where I can be myself,
A place that I can eat.

Safe is what I feel,
Pets I can stroke,
Warm and clean and comfy,
A place full of hope.

Jemma Dique (11)
The Matthew Arnold School, Staines

A Tiger's Ideal Home

My ideal home would be,
One where the lion looks up to me,
One where I wear the crown,
I'll show him the door, the infernal clown!
He thinks he's cool, he thinks he's hip,
Until someone gets out the good ol' catnip!
I deserve to be the king of the jungle,
That would be the ideal home for me!

Lewis Demmon (12)
The Matthew Arnold School, Staines

My Ideal Home

My home is a place to relax.
My house is full of knick-knacks.
My home is a place where I feel safe.
My home is a warm place.
In my house I am surrounded by my family.
Home is where I can blurt things out randomly.

Alex Hanson (12)
The Matthew Arnold School, Staines

My Ideal Home

My ideal home is made of chocolate.
It is almost impossible to double lock it.
Along with the chocolate walls,
Are the guitar doors.
With a thousand inch TV, is a sofa made from footballs
And in this house there are no rules.
My garden goes on forever and so will my house
And on the bottom floor there is not even the smallest mouse.

Zeyn Sadiq (11)
The Matthew Arnold School, Staines

My Ideal Home

Home is a place
A place to play
A place to sing
A place you can be yourself
A place you just let your worries go away
A home is your family
Your life
Your home.

Phoebe Saville (11)
The Matthew Arnold School, Staines

Snail House

My ideal home is right on my back
It's warm and it's cosy so I choose when I want a nap
It's got all my belongings, it makes me feel safe
Even though it's small to me it's a big space
It's got lots of furniture, I have everything I need
My house may only be a shell but it's all I need.

Rebecca Aldred (13)
The Matthew Arnold School, Staines

My Home

M y home is . . .
Y ummy dinners

H ome to me and my family
O utstandingly clean
M odern furniture
E verything I could ever want!

I love my home!

Katie Clarke (12)
The Matthew Arnold School, Staines

My House

M y house is the best
Y asmine, my friend, loves it

H olly, my sister, jumps around in it
O llie, my dog, sleeps in it
U gly is the wrong word to describe it
S am the man plays in it
E veryone likes my house.

Ben Castleman (12)
The Matthew Arnold School, Staines

My Ideal Home!

My ideal home would balance on a cone,
I wonder if the neighbours would moan!
With chocolate and strawberry ice cream on top,
I'll have to hope the weather's not too hot,
Because if it is and the ice cream melts away
I'll just have to make a new one another day!

Rosie Saunders (12)
The Matthew Arnold School, Staines

Fear

Children scared, beyond despair
They search for help but no one cares
The hurt endured, the horrors faced
All their lives a constant chase
Unable to run, nowhere to hide
Nobody there in which to confide.

Jessica Ketchen
The Matthew Arnold School, Staines

Hello Again

Hello again, my old friend,
Now, where have you been?
Time has passed so silently
Since you last were seen.

Have you been down the brook?
Or to some castle, far, far away?
Did you go visit your dying gran
And make amends on her last day?

Life has been so peaceful,
Since you last were here,
The days have faded gently,
My dreams restful and clear.

I almost thought you were dead;
You were gone so long!
I almost held a funeral;
A celebration of dance and song.

But no, no, you were here all along,
I don't think you ever left.
You lurked just below my skin
Dancing gleefully with death.

Waiting for me to forget my fear
Just behind my eye,
Reminding me always:
You are here till I die.

Rachel Tookey (17)
The Tiffin Girls' School, Kingston-upon-Thames

Mrs Wolhuter - My English Teacher

Dear Mrs Wolhuter,
What shall I do?
English is hard
I haven't got a clue!

Write a little poem, dear
Make it rhyme and regard
Include lots of punctuation
It can't be very hard.

Dear Mrs Wolhuter,
What will you say?
Geography is difficult
It makes the day so grey.

It's all mountains and lakes, dear
Plus, all the rest
No matter what you learn or think
English is the best!

Dear Mrs Wolhuter,
French is such a stress!
Je ne parle le Français
Tomorrow I have a test!

Write it out in English first
Then you can translate
But grammar is a preference, dear
From which you can create.

Dear Mrs Wolhuter,
Science is a blast!
One boy burnt his eyebrows off
It happened very fast!

Science is confusing, dear
Newton metre or mass
Still, English is much better
I know that you will pass.

Dear Mrs Wolhuter,
Maths is a struggle
For I don't know any answers, Miss
It's like I have to juggle.

Stop, stop, stop!
What don't you get?
I am in English
And maths makes me sweat.

Rosie Upton [13]
Thornden School, Eastleigh

The Silence

A shot, a tear, a cry
More people die
A body on the road
Still as a toad

Silence falls
In the echoing halls
Crows circling in the sky
Watching people die

A crash, a scream, a bash
Silence leaves an utter
Better the silence
For it leaves like a flutter

A growl, a moan, a groan
Hoping to go home
Death is near
With chilling fear

A whimper, a moan, a slash
Silence in the hut
A crash, bang, bash
Fire turns to ash

All things die
But do not try.

Adam Rogers [12]
Thornden School, Eastleigh

One Last Breath

Our eyes met across
The classroom.
I winked at him
And blew him a kiss,
Ducking my head
With Californian blond hair.

She winked at me,
She winked at me!
I think, over the moon
With love.
The prettiest girl in the
Whole school,
Wants me to be her date.

I've got him hooked,
Let's reel him in
To give him a shocking surprise.

Six o'clock that evening,
At the deserted park street
I think:
Tom, you're a lucky dude.

Lip gloss? Check.
Silky, shiny hair? Check.
Murderous weapon? Of course.

Swagger across the park,
Boy, you've got this in your hands.
There she is, as glamorous as ever.

Lean in for a kiss and . . .
Lean in for a kiss and . . .

I gasped
Blood poured
She smiled.

He gasped
I stared
And smiled.

Lauren Baverstock (14)
Thornden School, Eastleigh

A Hanging Key . . .

She walked and walked,
'Til she could walk no more,
A table,
A chair,
But not a door.

A window that was locked
And a hanging key,
She reached to grab it,
Why shouldn't she?

She opened the window,
But to her despair,
She had unleashed,
Her worst nightmare . . .

All massive with sharp teeth,
All fat and round,
He roared and stomped
And shook the ground.

She ran and ran,
'Til she could run no more,
No table,
No chair,
But her bedroom door . . .

Alexandra Hopwood (13)
Thornden School, Eastleigh

Freedom

I want to know what it feels like to be free
For someone to finally appreciate me
And inside I'm scared, I'm petrified
I'm alive now but feel dead inside

The Germans are near
Coming closer I fear
I want to know why
They want me to die

My parents are gone
Their smiles, they shone
But now my sky is dark and grey
No more to see a happier day

I know now my time is ticking
And the feeling of hurt is slowly sticking
No one here to comfort me
And now I finally see

The Germans are here
To fill me with fear
I want to know why
They wanted me to die.

Katy Rowledge (12)
Thornden School, Eastleigh

Lost And Never Found!

The horror and the pain,
    Death is not a game,
Starving and thirsty,
    Dirty and trapped.
Everything has been taken from us,
    And we can't get it back.

Lisa Wright (13)
Thornden School, Eastleigh

This Is Not My World (WWII)

Alone, frightened, hurt.
Taking,
What does not belong to them.
Destruction,
Killing people beside me.
Help,
This is not my world,
It has turned
Into something that is wrong.
Evil,
Around every corner.
Sorrow,
In people's eyes.
I'm a child,
Stuck.
Help,
This is not my world!

Amy Crockford (13)
Thornden School, Eastleigh

The Deadly Trance

I was floating,
Floating in my own world,
Unable to breathe,
Hoping,
Hoping someone would break the surface,
Begging,
Begging to breathe again,
Begging to break free from this constant trance,
I was scared,
I was drowning . . .

Bryony Peters (12)
Thornden School, Eastleigh

Fearer

It creeps, it crawls,
It watches your every move.
It can prey on the weak,
It can prey on the strong,
The proud or the protective,
Like a silent killer yet it uses instinct, emotion, as a life support.
It is never visible, yet at times it seems to whisper to you,
Like it is about to grasp you with its bony fingers
And pull you into an abyss.
However, this creature is a phony,
Playing on the minds of both children and adults.
On the ground, in the sea or even in the air.
It has a name, but describe it you cannot, for its name is Fear.
And Fear can haunt you until the end, like a ghost watching you.
So do not be sucked into the trap of fear,
Because once you fall into it, you have to dig yourself out . . .

Finlay Naylor (11)
Thornden School, Eastleigh

Afghanistan

Listen up, I wanna say this,
Barack Obama is part of this,
He's gonna have a plan for the Taliban,
Cos the USA want to go to Iran.

There's already been too much harm,
It's turning out to be another Vietnam,
The boys in blue are from the UN,
Let's finish this war in 2010.

Let's put an end to this mess,
We need to decide what is best,
No more killing, no more deceased,
It's vital that we live in peace.

James Elliott (12)
Thornden School, Eastleigh

Seasons

Hot and gives you a tan, nothing like the sun
Games with friends in the sun, nothing like fun
Getting up late and going to bed later, nothing like summer

Leaves are falling, lining the floor
Nothing like the colours
Start of school, seeing friends, nothing like friends
Not too hot but not too cold, nothing like autumn.

Snow is falling, getting days off school
Nothing like snow
Hot chocolate on Christmas morning, nothing like Christmas
Snowball fights, then warm hot chocolate, nothing like winter

New chicks spring out of their eggs, nothing like new life
Flowers waking after their two season nap, nothing like the colours
Sunny weather, wearing what you like, nothing like spring.

Kirsty McCulloch (12)
Thornden School, Eastleigh

Braces

Children are like braces, in many different ways
You seem to sometimes need them, but not really want them,
They do lots of harm, but mostly do well,
And are put in difficult places, that pull and nag and grip,
Children are like braces; they are new and full of surprises,
They stand out because of size, or simply just blend in,
They can affect the way that people look,
And make you talk in different tones.
Children are like braces in many different ways,
They are in life for a purpose - and make people pleased,
You do not wish to share them,
But when their time is up,
They leave you standing proudly,
Smiling till you drop.

Lydia Pallot (12)
Thornden School, Eastleigh

My Doctor Gave Me Some Bullets And Said, 'Take One For Depression . . . '

I killed a man today, and the after party was atrocious.

We stripped his apartment bare like trees in winter, puffing out the objects lurking in his bedroom like guilty candles, while his mother watched with speechless indignation.

Lurching down the motorway, we took them to the dump, with a suffocating cloud of unfathomable guilt lingering overhead.

Blame spread like a moral cancer - it was inevitable, like death - for I found no reason to justify his self-destruction.

Priests came and went, buzzing with insect-like malignancy, muttering clichés about depression, assuring us that it wasn't anybody's fault.

'When you're depressed,' they said, 'it feels like your soul is bleeding. Sometimes the easiest thing is to stick two fingers up at all creation and quit before nature fires you.'

Regardless, I've devised my own philosophy. Sometimes the proudest lion, who can roar long and loud when filled with arrows, can be killed by a mere shadow.

Life is madness, and somewhere in the back of every head is a rough patch that longs for the jolt of a bullet.

Better to die now, before we lose more blood!

Death winds his clocks indiscriminately, and they strike at the palaces of kings and the hovels of the poor.

Nonetheless, a smothering bleakness choked us at the funeral.

They tied his fists in knots and coated them with luscious bespoke fabric; a desperate shot at transforming a slab of dead meat back into a person.

News of his death spread like a disease, throbbing through the media.

An awful plague of journalists descended, writhing like vipers with wires and bulbous cameras, so I shrunk away into his aged house.

Justice is like water; it washes people clean. Stumbling through those ancient rooms, picturing him, up to his lips in poverty and generally wretched, I failed to grasp the swollen injustice of it all.

Outside, his mother tearfully plated neglect with gold, teasing herself into the assumption that it wasn't her fault.

I know what depression is: a terminal illness that switches brimming crowds of people into lifeless galleries, cools laughter to a dry leaf blowing in the wind, and makes the bounty of the universe flat and profitless.

You don't want bother, you just want to sleep. I remember that in class he liked to daydream; for a couple of moments he could have the life he wanted, before opening his eyes to reality. Locked inside the coffin, his corpse shrivelled at the grotesque indignity of it all, and I don't blame him. When I lose a friend, a part of me dies, and the best part. But good on him for clawing through the wall all nature scratches its nails against; the mark he left on me assures me that he marches forth to enter with applause. Perhaps his rotten corpse shall sprout into a tree, so part of that forgotten world he shall forever be, with space raining his stars eternally.

And here's me, plunging back through bruise-skied insomnia, free-falling through darkness, tumbling across acres of empty space, singing to myself, 'No way but this, no way but this . . . '

Darren Mindham (16)
Wilson's School, Wallington

Freedom

The chains are heavy,
The chains are tight.
They are on both
Day and night.

The machines are huge,
The machines are loud.
How can my parents
Ever be proud.

I wish that I
Could go to school
And not live under
The slave master's rule.

I wish I was
In the UK
The children there
Can laugh and play.

So next time
You go out to play
Just remember
It's not all that way.

Martin Lindill (12)
Woodland Middle School, Bedford

Food O Food

Food o food
When you have fed me
There's apples and apricots
All for me.

Food o food
When you have fed me
There's beef and bacon
All for me.

Food o food
When you have fed me
There's carrot and cake
All for me

Food o food
When you have fed me
There's duck and doughnuts
All for me

Food o food
When you have fed me
There's éclairs and eggs
All for me

Food o food
When you have fed me
There's figs and fish
All for me

Food o food
When you have fed me
There's grapes and goose
All for me

Food o food
When you have fed me
There's ham and honey
All for me

Food o food
When you have fed me
There's ice cream and icing
All for me

Food o food
When you have fed me
There's jam and Jaffa cakes
All for me

Food o food
When you have fed me
There's kiwi and ketchup
All for me

Food o food
When you have fed me
There's lollies and lettuce
All for me

Food o food
When you have fed me
There's mango and melon
All for me

Food o food
When you have fed me
There's nuts and noodles
All for me

Food o food
When you have fed me
There's oranges and olives
All for me

Food o food
When you have fed me
There's pizza and pasta
All for me

Food o food
When you have fed me
There's quiche and quenelle
All for me

Food o food
When you have fed me
There's rice and ribs
All for me

Food o food
When you have fed me
There's salmon and Smarties
All for me

Food o food
When you have fed me
There's tuna and toast
All for me

Food o food
When you have fed me
There's ugli fruit and udo
All for me

Food o food
When you have fed me
There's veal and vanilla
All for me

Food o food
When you have fed me
There's walnut and wafers
All for me

Food o food
When you have fed me
There's xigue and xylitol
All for me

Food o food
When you have fed me
There's yoghurt and yolk
All for me

Food o food
When you have fed me
There's zumba and zatar
All for me.

Thomas Herbert (12)
Woodland Middle School, Bedford

My Cat, My Cat

My cat called Marley
Is a sweet black cat,
He has a blue collar,
Marley likes having cuddles.

My cat, my cat,
As sweet as sugar,
Always wanting love,
They like getting gifts.

My cat called Pearl
Is a sweet black and white cat,
She doesn't have a collar,
But she likes being adventurous.

My cat, my cat,
Big and bushy,
Always making me proud,
They make me love them so much.

My cat called Misty
Is a sweet white cat,
She doesn't like collars,
But she likes being in calm places.

My cat, my cat,
As sweet as sugar,
Always wanting love,
They like getting gifts.

My cat called Sweep
Is a sweet black and white cat,
He hasn't got a collar,
But he likes playing.

My cat, my cat,
Big and bushy,
Always making me proud,
They make me love them so much.

My cat called Jet,
She is a black cat with a white line on her belly,
She has a green collar,
But she likes crying and being annoying.

My cat, my cat,
As sweet as sugar,
Always wanting love,
They like getting gifts.

My cat called Shadow
Is a sweet black cat with a small white stripe down her chest,
She doesn't have a collar,
But she always purrs when she hugs her dad Phil.

My cat, my cat,
All big and bushy,
Always making me proud,
They make me so happy when they are around me.

My cat called Ziggy
Is a sweet ginger cat with white paws,
He does not have a collar because they annoy him,
He loves everyone and everything especially hugs.

My cat, my cat,
As sweet as sugar,
Always wanting love,
And they always get love.

My cat Mitch
Is a sweet black cat with white paws,
He doesn't have a collar because he is very old,
But he has his old days and his kitten days.

My cat, my cat,
All big and bushy,
Always making me proud,
They make me so happy when they are around me.

My cat Max
Is a sweet tabby who is brown, black and grey,
He doesn't have a collar because he is old,
But he hates having his belly rubbed.

My cat, my cat,
As sweet as sugar,
Always wanting love,
And they get love all the time along with gifts.

My cat Floyd,
Is a white dwarf cat with hardly any fur,
He doesn't have a collar because they make him itch
But he likes cuddling into you at night.

My cat, my cat,
All big and bushy.
Always making me proud,
They make me so happy when they are around me.

It upsets me when things happen to them,
I like watching my cats grow up.

Kerry Meredith (12)
Woodland Middle School, Bedford

Important To Me

Important to me
To me
What I like. What I don't.
Cheese and cake and both together
My clothes, socks, pants and the weather.

Drawing and painting and sketching in art
My book I possess with great care and heart.
Yellow, bright pink, orange and blue
My favourite collection of the one same shoe.

I like odd numbers, three and nine
As if those odds are actually mine.
Books, DVDs, no books, DVDs
Harry Potter and Cat in the Hat, from books to DVDs.

My room has green walls, blue wardrobe, white door
A picture, a clock and a fake lollipop.
So colours, my room, cheesecake and art
Odd numbers are fine like three and nine.

Alex Sanderson (12)
Woodland Middle School, Bedford

Wilbur

Wilbur, since he was an egg, was mine
Lying in the corner of the room.
He was just a little orange ball
But I know he would hatch soon.
I woke up one morning
And I was shocked to see
Several hundred baby spiders
Some crawling over me.
After I had told my mum
They were all but gone.
I looked around but could not see
A single, tiny one.
I looked under books
And under my bed
But they had all vanished,
Some probably dead.
A few days later, I forgot
The strange day's great event.
I had, you see, just finished school
And naturally, home I went.
I looked in the corner of my room
And saw some orange flecks.
Then those vivid memories
Returned to then connect.
I looked up to my ceiling
And saw two small arachnids.
'Wilbur,' I decided,
'And the other one is Agnes,'
But, soon, the girl had disappeared.
Wilbur was all I had.
He hadn't moved since the first day
I thought him to be sad.
Then, I had a dreadful thought
And lightly tapped his head.
Then my suspicions were confirmed,
Poor Wilbur was dead.

Charlie Hughes (11)
Woodland Middle School, Bedford

My Cat, My Cat

My cat called Marley
Is a sweet black cat,
He has a blue collar,
Marley likes having cuddles.

My cat, my cat,
As sweet as sugar,
Always wanting love,
They like getting gifts.

My cat called Pearl
Is a sweet black and white cat,
She doesn't have a collar,
But she likes being adventurous.

My cat, my cat,
Big and bushy,
Always making me proud,
They make me love them so much.

My cat called Misty
Is a sweet white cat,
She doesn't like collars,
But she likes being in calm places.

My cat, my cat,
As sweet as sugar,
Always wanting love,
They like getting gifts.

My cat called Sweep
Is a sweet black and white cat,
He hasn't got a collar,
But he likes playing.

My cat, my cat,
Big and bushy,
Always making me proud,
They make me love them so much.

My cat called Jet,
She is a black cat with a white line on her belly,
She has a green collar,

But she likes crying and being annoying.

My cat, my cat,
As sweet as sugar,
Always wanting love,
They like getting gifts.

My cat called Shadow
Is a sweet black cat with a small white stripe down her chest,
She doesn't have a collar,
But she always purrs when she hugs her dad Phil.

My cat, my cat,
All big and bushy,
Always making me proud,
They make me so happy when they are around me.

My cat called Ziggy
Is a sweet ginger cat with white paws,
He does not have a collar because they annoy him,
He loves everyone and everything especially hugs.

My cat, my cat,
As sweet as sugar,
Always wanting love,
And they always get love.

My cat Mitch
Is a sweet black cat with white paws,
He doesn't have a collar because he is very old,
But he has his old days and his kitten days.

My cat, my cat,
All big and bushy,
Always making me proud,
They make me so happy when they are around me.

My cat Max
Is a sweet tabby who is brown, black and grey,
He doesn't have a collar because he is old,
But he hates having his belly rubbed.

My cat, my cat,
As sweet as sugar,
Always wanting love,
And they get love all the time along with gifts.

My cat Floyd,
Is a white dwarf cat with hardly any fur,
He doesn't have a collar because they make him itch
But he likes cuddling into you at night.

My cat, my cat,
All big and bushy.
Always making me proud,
They make me so happy when they are around me.

It upsets me when things happen to them,
I like watching my cats grow up.

Kerry Meredith (12)
Woodland Middle School, Bedford

What Matters To Me

A friend is someone to laugh with,
To joke with, to share with.
A friend is someone to encourage,
Be encouraged by.
Having a friend matters to me.

A family is loving, caring,
They will not let you down,
They will love you whatever you do.
My family matters to me.

A pet is something to play with,
To care for, to love.
Having a pet matters to me.

My room is a special place,
You can make it your own,
You can retreat to it when you feel insecure.
A room is exactly what you want it to be.
My room is my special place and it matters to me.

Alex Evans (12)
Woodland Middle School, Bedford

Hair Matters To Me

What matters to me?
Few people query
What does matter to me?
And rather smugly,
I say,
Hair.
Hair,
People say.
Yes hair.
Weird.
No; listen
Hair is like life
You can do nothing with it,
Make nothing with it,
But! Don't worry about it too much,
It can't give you what you give it.
It has a personality.
That's going too far!
Listen!
It can be jumpy,
It can be wavy,
You can have wacky hair,
Or no hair!
That's very boring.
Blond, brown, brunette, black
It comes in all different shapes and sizes,
This is why hair matters to me,
Cos it's just,
Like
Life.

Louis Brown (12)
Woodland Middle School, Bedford

What Matters To Me

Music makes me free my mind,
It makes me believe,
Makes me think,
It's how I feel.

I think of how I feel,
I just want to let go,
Let people know,
It's how I feel.

I see it in colours,
Deep and solid,
It excites me,
It's how I feel.

I think of what I feel,
I just want to let go,
Let people know,
It's how I feel.

I emit myself,
In my interest and passion,
It makes me emotive,
It's how I feel.

I think of how I feel,
I just want to let go,
Let people know,
It's how I feel.

There's too many feelings to express,
I'm indecisive,
I just want to stand and shout,
It's how I feel.

I think of how I feel,
I just want to let go,
Let people know,
It's how I feel.

The lyrics make sense,
I understand,
The portraying emotion,

It's how I feel.

I think of how I feel,
I just want to let go,
Let people know,
That's how I feel.

Lucy Pedder (12)
Woodland Middle School, Bedford

To Be Free!

I want to be, forever free;
Never any imprisoning bars for me;
I can't describe, describe how I feel inside;
To be free, free, forever free;
Free as an eagle soaring high in the sky;
Free for the whole of my life and that's no lie.

I want to be, forever free;
Never enclosed, where I don't want to be;
I can't describe, describe how I feel inside;
To be free, free, forever free;
Free as a star shining bright on high;
Free my whole life and that you can't buy.

I want to be, forever free;
Never closed in, no darkness for me;
I can't describe, describe how I feel inside;
To be free, free, forever free;
Free as the wind blowing, through a ripe field of hay;
Free my whole life, until my dying day.

Free to say whatever I please;
Sailing through life with grace and ease;
Nobody holding me back;
My life back on track;
My body is free;
My mind is free;
I am free.

Thomas Woodcraft (12)
Woodland Middle School, Bedford

Me!

Me!
Michael Frost, I love all my family
Me!
Nobody knows who I will be
Me!
When I tell jokes people giggle with glee
Me!
I love to be by the sea
Me!
I love all my possessions you see
Me!
Elephants, my favourite animal and will forever be
Me!
I'm very friendly and have two fish who are silvery
Me!
I have a dad, the best is he
Me!
I have a mum, the best is she
Me!
I have a sister, the worst is she
Me!
I have some hobbies and they would be . . .
Me!
I like to climb a tree
Me!
I like to play football, whoopee
Me!
I play tennis you see
Me!
I also like to eat curry
Me!
I am quite brainy
Me!
My cousin has a dog called Barney, my bed is very cosy
Me!
My friend Ed is a goalie
Me!
I'm quite healthy and my house is where I live but my parents have thirty

Me!
I am very jolly and my favourite food is a pea
Me!
I like the band Bon Jovi, I eat lots of food for tea
Me!
My favourite weather is snowy, I never met either granny
Me!
I am tiny. Brothers I do not have any
Me!
I'd like to win the Euro lottery and learn karate
That's all from me!

Michael Frost (11)
Woodland Middle School, Bedford

My Mum Is The Best

I love my mum, she is the best.
She scores goals but always tries her best.
Mum takes me shopping and always busy me stuff,
We love shopping.
She is always there for me when I'm upset
Or I have hurt myself.
Sometimes she takes me to the cinema
And we go nearly every month.
I love her with all my heart
From deep down in my heart.
She loves me with all her heart.
If I had to choose the best mum
She would be the best mum.
Mum has always got a smile on her face.
Mum and Dad always say to me and my sister,
'Have you had a good day at school?'
She is fantastic and fun, creative and good to have a laugh with,
That's why my mum's the best.

Jessica Hutchinson (12)
Woodland Middle School, Bedford

Music

Music, music fills my ears,
Helps us conquer and face our fears,
Sometimes emotional and can bring us to tears,
That's what music is about.

Sometimes loud, sometimes quiet,
Sometimes it may even cause a riot,
If you don't know you should try it,
That's what music is about.

Music can be played in bands,
Listened to by screaming fans,
Showing support through feet and hands,
That's what music is about.

Music's like flowers: they die over time,
It's evil and exciting and can cause a lot of crimes
And finds the real person in front of you,
That's what music is about.

Songs have lyrics that may be upsetting,
Sad and cold and maybe depressing,
Some may write as they are confessing,
That's what music is about.

Music makes you want to dance,
Makes you want to leap and prance,
Sits back and listen to the music.

The music can hear you too.

Millie De Kauwe (12)
Woodland Middle School, Bedford

The Fear

The fear
Of everything I wanted
Of all my dreams coming true
Or the world turning bright blue
Of family being hurt
Or falling straight in the dirt
Of losing fantastic friends
Of having lots of split ends
Of suffering from sadness
Or being lonely and homeless.

The fear
Of being so very near
My mind makes it really clear
The fear
Of thunderstorms and lightning
It's incredibly frightening
The fear
Of drowning in the deep sea
The fear of just being me
The fear of driving a jeep
Of prices that aren't too cheap
The fear of rocking the boat
Or falling into the moat

This is what fear means to me!

Lauren Ash (12)
Woodland Middle School, Bedford

Open The Door

When I open my door I see my dog's paw.
A smile on her face.
She scratches and brushes and bruises,
Whines but that's alright because she's mine.
Leaving her some days is upsetting,
I love her so much when I scratch her on the scruff.
I love her, she's my doggy.
I love all the hugs, love all the kisses.
She has to eat bones, pencils and also phones.
She plays with her toys, shocks all the boys.
But I love her, she's my doggy.
I love all the hugs, love all the kisses.
I walk her at night, sometimes at day.
My mum says the magic word
And she's off like a lion chasing a lamb.
Into the kitchen loud and tapping her paws.
At night-time now I hear her howl
Knowing it's the 9pm bark.
She sleeps like a baby moving her long legs.
She's a brindle you know, full Irish greyhound from head to paw.
I love her and she loves me
And that's why she's special to me.

Hannah Tyler (12)
Woodland Middle School, Bedford

Christmas

Christmas, best day of the year.
Love, joy, happiness,
Santa dropping off pressies,
Children waking up screaming with a cheer.
All the dads gather and drink some beer.
Eating up the turkey and leaving some behind,
Can't wait to go outside!

Jodie Darvall (11)
Woodland Middle School, Bedford

What Matters To Me?

Happiness is me,
Happiness is you,
Happiness is all the things
That we love to do.

Happiness is freedom,
Happiness is unity,
Happiness is priceless,
Used in our community.

Happiness is smiles,
Happiness is love,
Happiness is all the things
You see up above.

Happiness is family,
Happiness is friends,
Happiness is all the things
You do on weekends.

Happiness is fruit,
Happiness is veg,
Happiness is all the blackberries
Along the garden hedge.

Jake Shawe (12)
Woodland Middle School, Bedford

My Horse

My horse is white
My horse is right
My horse will bite
My horse runs like the wind
If you are kind
She will not bite
My horse is interesting!

Trudie Reardon (13)
Woodland Middle School, Bedford

Friendship

My friendship is my heart
For that will never be apart.
Friends are like a sister or a brother
We fight but still love each other.

We talk like there's no tomorrow
So there's always something to borrow
From house to house we always go
Telling stuff that makes us go whoo!

As we shop around the clock
We don't ever, ever stop
Every single day we laugh
Even on the phone or in the bath.

Friendship to me is all I need
Is that OK or is that greed?
I want to have fun with my friends
Helping them when they're on the mends.

Friends are loyal when you're down
They make you laugh like a clown
My friendship is my heart
For that will never be apart!

Sasha Ralević (12)
Woodland Middle School, Bedford

Technology

Technology is a must have for me.
I'll never go a day without it.
Xbox, computer, PS3, anything will do.
Me and my friends love to play them.
Any day of the week, will do for me.
Early, morning, late night, middle of the day doesn't matter.
Since I was seven I loved to play them.

George Roberts (12)
Woodland Middle School, Bedford

226

Pat The Cat

There was a cat
And he lived in a hat
He didn't like rats
And was terrified of bats
His name is Pat
And he sleeps on a mat

He had a mother
But he didn't have a brother
And still didn't have a secret lover
Then his mother
Fell down a drain

It started to rain
And she was in pain
She climbed up
Then fell down again
Then poor Pat was ashamed

Pat didn't have a mother
And still didn't have a brother
Poor Pat lived with the rats, bats
And had no mat.

Regan Ovendale (12)
Woodland Middle School, Bedford

Chocolate

Chocolate, inviting brown
Chocolate trickles down my throat
Chocolate, one bite and you'll adore
Dark, white, milk, strawberry, mint and orange
Chocolate's luscious flavours
Chocolate enters my mouth mmm heaven
When melted my tastebuds tingle
Chocolate matters to me, we couldn't be apart.

Gemma Scott (11)
Woodland Middle School, Bedford

Friends

Friends are everything, without them
We would be alone, bewildered, have nothing at all,
You might sit and cry in the hall,
No one to support us, no shoulder to lean on,
No one to cry to when your pet has just died,
They would stop that,
You would feel happier inside,
That you would have friends to help,
So you won't scream and yelp.

At school you might play together
Or chat and gossip and have a laugh,
Even a sleepover, eat all the popcorn,
Watch a movie, but without friends none of that, oh no.
No fun anymore, no sleepovers, MSN or Facebook
No one to chat to
So think . . .
Remember you're not a kid forever!

Rebecca Mair (11)
Woodland Middle School, Bedford

Grandad!

Grandad
Louis Chadwick, mine
Kind, loving, supportive, warm, a strong heart.

Always there for me
Always helps me with my homework
Teaches me golf? I love it!

You might not be around for much longer
But while he's here, I want to tell you something
I love you!

Grandad!

Jack James (11)
Woodland Middle School, Bedford

What Matters To Me?

When I am sailing
I am usually in a race,
Going at such a fast pace.
Sometimes going up and down
As a motor boat
Comes speeding round.

Sometimes I am winning
I am ahead of the race,
Going along at such a fast pace.
As I cross the finish line
I get a toot on the horn,
The other boats, far behind, look like grains of corn.

What matters to me
Might not matter to you
But I like sailing
So that's what I do.

Thomas Lark [12]
Woodland Middle School, Bedford

It Don't Matter!

It don't matter if you play football on a bad team
It don't matter if you go to after school clubs
It don't matter if you go out with your friends
And do something embarrassing
It don't matter in school you are in low sets for everything
It don't matter if you read
It don't matter if you get the highest or lowest level in the class
But it does matter if you do drugs
It does matter if you are smoking
Think you are killing yourself
And I don't want certain things happening to you!

Katie Manners [12]
Woodland Middle School, Bedford

What Matters To Me?

What matters to me
Is not as small as a bee,
Or as big as a tree.

Horses are what matter to me,
Their movement is free.
Like moving over liquid,
Like running over water.

Their strength, power, love
Holds magnificent beauty.
Horses run fast, horses run free,
With such power amazing to me.

The wildness of a new horse,
It's raging, mad, beastly power.
It captures me,
The way they're free.

Hannah Burdett (12)
Woodland Middle School, Bedford

What Does Matter?

What does matter?
Learning, success, money?
Knowledge, nature, life?
Rest, equality, peace, spirit?
Whatever . . .
You may think that the most important things is a colour -
Green, like a leaf.
But when the end comes and the lights go out,
All that's left is belief.
Yes, when we're old and we've lost all our teeth . . .
All that's left is belief.

Dom Maelzer (11)
Woodland Middle School, Bedford

Manchester United

Man United make me smile with their skill
That's so versatile.

Manchester United, their players' talent
And skill to make fans feel their thrill.

Manchester's stadium is like a home with the other fans
And players united to make other teams play pandemonium.

After they play us, Chelsea, Man City and Liverpool
Will never ever be cool.

Park Ji Sung he's the best,
Back of the net just like the rest.

Van der Sar like a pro,
Never lets the ball go.

Oliver Barker [11]
Woodland Middle School, Bedford

The Lightning Struck Tree
By The Little Stream

If you venture down the fields of barley and wheat,
You shall come to a queer little bridge,
Almost falling apart, rotting wood and worms,
Under that is a quickly flowing stream,
Fathoms deep and full of sharks, at least that's what it seems.
If they leap and catch you, you have only a minute to leap from
Their humongous jaws and stop yourself from drowning,
If you look to the opposite bank you will see a hollow tree,
Lost in the shrouds of time, only I can see its true value,
A rope swing above the stream,
A den for treasure from the seven seas,
A sniper post for peashooters and slingshots.

James Tobin [11]
Woodland Middle School, Bedford

Hope

You need hope to stay strong,
Hope to stay wise
But it will always be by your side.

When you feel good,
When you feel bad,
If you have hope you won't be sad.

If you want to succeed,
If you want to achieve,
If you have hope you can do all these.

If you keep hope in your mind,
You will find,
You can achieve your dreams.

Vicky Haimes (12)
Woodland Middle School, Bedford

My Friends And Me

Friends, friends they are so cool
And we go to Woodland School
We go to the park every day
Just to go and play, play, play!

Then it's time to go home
I have my dinner and text on my phone
Then it's time to go to bed
And I lie down my head
Then my mum says goodnight
After I turn out the light.

Jade Burles (12)
Woodland Middle School, Bedford

My Room

My room is a bright homely green,
It has crystal white furniture and a stripy green bed,
A luxury lamp with wild floral patterns
And curtains that hang droopily by the sunlight,
Where I love to spend most of my life.

My room is my own little planet,
A place happy and peaceful at all times,
Where I play my electric guitar,
That echoes through the house,
Where it matters to me.

Lucy Guerrero (11)
Woodland Middle School, Bedford

What Matters To Me?

What matters to me, friends, things that just might never end.
It all counts on how much time I spend.
Personality points me towards individuality,
All part of my lifestyle . . .
Me.

My teddy collection that always glows, with perfection, wow!
My family are the most important aspect,
All loving, all caring, regardless.
What matters to me is my lifestyle . . .
Me.

Lois Johnson (12)
Woodland Middle School, Bedford

Friends, Friends

Friends, friends they're always there,
Friends, friends don't share your secrets,
Friends, friends don't let you down,
Friends, friends make you laugh,
Friends, friends spend time together,
Friends, friends they stick up for you,
Friends, friends they come and go
But the ones that stay are the ones that glow.

I love my friends!

Mei-Ann Bartram (11)
Woodland Middle School, Bedford

Friends

Friends make my world go round,
Keeping me happy, keeping me sound.

They tell me if something doesn't look good,
That's what a true friend would do.

They pick me up when I am down,
They're the ones keeping my feet on the ground.

An opportunity for a friend like this,
Is an opportunity that you shouldn't miss.

Emily Potts (11)
Woodland Middle School, Bedford

No Matter

No matter how hard I try
There will never be praise.
No matter how much I care
I will always be blamed.
No matter how famous I grow,
I will never be happy.
No matter how old I turn out to be,
My life,
Will end in sorrow.

Ross Knight (13)
Woodland Middle School, Bedford

Food, Food

Food, food o how I love you
Food, food I can have two
Pasta or chilli it's up to me
Food, food I can have tea!

Drink, drink o how I love you
Drink, drink I can have two
Coke or Sprite it's up to me
Drink, drink I need a pee!

Elliott Griffett (12)
Woodland Middle School, Bedford

Army Cadets

Air rifle, air rifle, I use air rifles
Left, right, left, right, left, right, left
Up and down the drill hall we go on parade
Left, right, left, right, left, we all go
In uniform every Monday and Wednesday

Drew Gillespie (12)
Woodland Middle School, Bedford

The Curry Song

Spicy, mild, cold and hot,
These are all my favourite pots.
What to do, what to do.
I will have some curry that's what I will do.

The humble curry, the humble curry,
I always eat it in a hurry.
Three pieces of naan bread, three pieces of naan bread,
The curry . . . it always gets inside my head.

Jack Sharp [12]
Woodland Middle School, Bedford

Wildcats!

Wildcats is our name.
Scoring goals is sometimes our game.
Our football kit is yellow and blue.
We give it all we've got,
But it doesn't matter cos that's what's important to me.

Wildcats try our hardest,
Even though we're the worst in the league,
But it don't matter cos that's what's important to me.

Rhianne Jones [12]
Woodland Middle School, Bedford

My Friends And Family

My friends make me smile,
My friends make me laugh,
My friends make me happy
When I am sad.

My family make me feel cared for,
My family make me feel special,
But my friends and family
Make me feel loved for who I am.

Georgia Fleet-Chapman (12)
Woodland Middle School, Bedford

Cool And Wicked

My Xbox is cool and wicked
I play it some days
It cost me £12.00
I play it all the way
The war game is exciting
Bullets fire from guns
Grenades make explosions
Causing lots of damage.

Ben Short (12)
Woodland Middle School, Bedford

My Cat

My cat is jet-black with emerald green eyes
That sparkle in the night.
She pounces at anything, even inanimate objects.
She claws and bites as she thinks she is a tiger cub
Hunting for her prey.
Everything fears her as she is my cat.

Karly Billimore (11)
Woodland Middle School, Bedford

Young Writers Information

We hope you have enjoyed reading this book - and that you will continue to enjoy it in the coming years.

If you like reading and writing poetry drop us a line, or give us a call, and we'll send you a free information pack.

Alternatively if you would like to order further copies of this book or any of our other titles, then please give us a call or log onto our website at www.youngwriters.co.uk

Young Writers Information
Remus House
Coltsfoot Drive
Peterborough
PE2 9BF
(01733) 890066